REIGNING AS ROYALTY
IN THE INNER LAND

BOOK I
KINGS AND QUEENS OF CREATION

LUC NIEBERGALL

Printed in the United States of America

First Edition, 2012

ISBN-10: 1478257857
ISBN-13: 978-1478257851

Kingdom Revelation Publishing

Dedication

I dedicate this book to my wife Eline who has always supported me in accomplishing my dreams with God. Never have I met a person who demonstrates what I teach in this book so well. I also dedicate this to my friends Steve Oh, Laura Oh and Lewis Ball who helped me with editing and publishing. Lastly, I dedicate this book to my family and friends at Imagine Church who have been a tremendous support and inspiration to me.

Endorsements

Reigning as Royalty in the Inner Land is a great read--
loaded with pertinent revelation concerning the things
God is doing in the earth today. I enjoyed it thoroughly
and found myself hungry to dig deeper into the truths
Luc was sharing and expounding upon. Spending time
with Luc and the team of people he's running with in
Calgary left me refreshed and excited for things to come
both in their region and in other parts of the globe.

Lance Jacobs
Associate Leader, Bethel Church
Redding, California

Too often the christian mystic is misunderstood by the
community of Christ-followers and when their eyes and
voices are needed most they cannot be found. Luc
Niebergall is a young, burgeoning mystic who loves and
follows Jesus Christ. Whether you agree with everything
in this book or not, you will certainly see and hear Luc's
passion for the Kingdom of Heaven.

Steve Osmond
Senior Pastor, First Assembly Church
The Green Light Initiative
Calgary, Alberta

Table of Contents

Introduction

I wrote this book believing that everyone who reads it will be released into a further revelation of who they are as sons and daughters of God. As the church we have at times walked in a poverty mindset, believing that we need to flee from darkness and hide in the club of Christianity until Jesus comes back to rescue us. Although we know that Jesus is coming back for a pure and spotless bride, many of us try to hide ourselves in a cloak of defeat, denying the world the opportunity to see the beauty that will draw them to Jesus. But, a revelation of the identity of the saints is about to be released across the globe which will bring the church to the centre stage of the world. The bride is about to stand in her new-found confidence, breaking out of her identity crisis. She will no longer sit feeling defeated and broken, but instead she will stand in her beauty to establish the order of heaven throughout the nations. This next move isn't about a one-man show or a great apostle or prophet stepping into his calling. This next move of the Spirit is about every saint standing in the fullness of their sonship, unashamed of their King Jesus and the kingdom of which they are citizens.

Just so that you know, I am aware that some of the things I say throughout this book may offend you, just as they once offended me. This is not my intention, however the fact remains that there are many around the world who are beginning to receive teachings that are very similar to the contents of this book you are about to read. I am also aware that some of you who read these teachings may be confronted by truths that are entirely new to you. Your theology may be challenged, but I encourage you not to dismiss what I say entirely. This book is a compilation of revelations that I have received from Holy Spirit in the past seven years concerning how to steward an internal revival. These revelations have transformed my very DNA. Just as quick as I am to advise you not to flippantly dismiss the words that I'm teaching, I also encourage you to not only take my word based on what I've written. If anything seems fresh and new to you, or if you feel sceptical about something that I've said, take it back to the Bible. As I write, it is my full intention to back everything that I say with the Word of God. My heart is to never stray from it. In the same way, my heart is to help expand your revelatory understanding of what was accomplished through the cross.

The kingdom is our paint and the world is our canvas. As co-creators with God we are given the privilege to dethrone drabness by establishing beauty.

Father right now I pray that Spirit of Wisdom and Revelation comes and rests upon every person who reads this book. Right now, I declare a revelatory impartation concerning true kingdom identity. Establish kingdom order within every heart. I release an impartation of understanding and power over every reader, freeing them to go further than I have ever dreamed for the purpose of revival.

The Kingdom

As we dive into things, we need to understand a foundational revelation. This revelation is one of the root truths that this next generation of Christians will live their lives from. When I use the term 'upcoming generation', I'm not just referring to those who are young as if the older will be forgotten in this movement. That couldn't be further from the truth. I am instead referring to those who are willing to be born into a new class of understanding. To understand is different than to know. Any intellectual can know, but in order for us to understand, we need to experience. This foundational revelation that is being restored is the truth of our inheritance as citizens of the kingdom of God. This revelation will be woven throughout the whole fabric of this book, so I encourage you to take the time to comprehend it in your spirit by meditating on the reality of what is being said as we continue to move forward together.

We will start off in Luke 11:2-4. Tradition tells us that this is the Lord's prayer, however it is important to note that Jesus wasn't even praying; He was instead teaching His disciples how they ought to pray. When Jesus' disciples came to ask Him how they should talk to the Father He spoke and said; "When you pray, say: Our Father in heaven, Hallowed be thy name. Your kingdom come. Your will be done on earth as it is in heaven." The word 'kingdom' that Jesus referred to here literally means 'kings domain'. If the kingdom is God's domain, then we know that wherever the kingdom of heaven is, that's where God is - it is His dwelling place. The culture of a household is always a reflection of the culture or personality of the One who has headship over it. Since God is heaven's creator, He is the head and authority of heaven which is His house. God in His very being is goodness and love. If heaven was God's expression in creation, we can be sure that its culture is a direct reflection of who God is.

Look back at what Jesus says in verse 2; "On earth as it is in heaven." Jesus was literally telling His disciples to pray that whatever was going on in heaven would be made manifest on earth. Jesus came to release a revelation that it was God's heart desire for the perfection of the culture of heaven to co-exist with creation on earth. Many of us have gotten off track in Jesus' true Kingdom message. A lot of us are living to see and experience heaven one day when we die, when it was Jesus' desire for us to experience the blessings of heaven now while we are still on earth. Ephesians 1:3 says; "Blessed be the God and Father of our Lord Jesus Christ, who has blessed us with every spiritual blessing in the heavenly places in Christ." This doesn't say that He will 'eventually' bless us with every spiritual blessing in heaven, it says He already has. He said "repent for the kingdom of heaven is at hand" (Matthew 4:17) saying that it is an attainable and tangible kingdom in hand's grasp. Heaven is in hand's grasp! This is good news! Jesus came to establish on earth a heavenly kingdom which functions out of heavenly principals here and now in our lives.

What are some principles of heaven? We know that the Bible says that in heaven there is no sickness, no disease, no depression, addictions or poverty. There is only perfect love, perfect health, peace, joy and abundant blessing. The kingdom of heaven is a place where God's will has complete rule and reign. When we receive Jesus as King we come under the rule and principals of His kingdom. We actually become citizens of heaven (Philippians 3:20). Sickness and addictions have no effect on us because they don't even exist in the kingdom that we are from. The Bible talks about two kingdoms; the kingdom of heaven (which is the kingdom of God) and the kingdom of darkness. When two kingdoms collide the greater kingdom will always prevail. A good example would be, say, if the kingdom of darkness had rule in an area of someone's life where they struggled with something like depression. When they receive Jesus as King in this area of their heart, His kingdom comes which is filled with perfect joy. Since God's kingdom is greater than the kingdom of darkness, His kingdom casts away depression, and joy becomes established in the individual's life.

One time when I was on a ministry trip I got the opportunity to speak at a meeting. Before I teach at a church I like to spend time with the Lord to ask Him what He has planned to do for the service. So I walked down a dirt road in the back country with Jesus and prepared my heart to listen. Immediately I began receiving a few words of knowledge for the meeting. He showed me that there would be a woman at the church who had a questionable lump under her rib cage on the lower right side, He spoke to me about someone who needed a creative miracle for their right hip and gave me a few more words of knowledge for healing. While I was writing these down in my journal I fell into an encounter with the Lord. Whether I was in the body or out of the body I don't actually know, but I was taken into heaven where I was standing amongst the clouds.

I looked to my left and saw a great angel standing about 10 feet away from me. Holy Spirit spoke to me and said, "Luc, watch what's about to happen." I looked and saw that beside the angel, stuck in the ground of heaven was a spear so unique that it demanded my attention. The spear glowed brilliantly and was clothed in intricate lightning bolts. Being only 10 feet away I was able to tell that there were designs inscribed across the spear. The patterns, pictures and words were so detailed they looked as though they were chiselled and crafted by the finest of tools. The angel reached down grabbing the spear with great confidence. As his grip tightened I could see pleasure on his face as strands of lightning from the spear overlapped his mighty hand. He lifted the spear out of the foundation of heaven and hurled it back into the ground beneath his feet. I was surprised to see that the spear didn't stick back into the ground. Instead it punctured right through heaven's floor in its entirety and exited heaven's atmosphere into the earth. I watched the spear soar ferociously through earth's sky. The small lightning bolts that ornamented the spear shone exuberantly on the intricately carved shaft in contrast to the foreboding lightning bolts that cracked across the dark mass of sky. My excitement grew as the spear descended, committed to find its destination. Finally approaching the end of its journey, I saw the spear racing towards the church that I was going to speak at. All of a sudden I was standing inside the church in the Spirit. I looked up anticipating the spear's arrival. Leaving no time for disappointment to sink in, it popped through the roof of the building leaving only a small hole in the ceiling. When the spear spiked into the ground, the floor of the church rippled, uprooting the foundation. After piercing the sanctuary's floor it stood as still and confident as when I first saw it in heaven. I walked hesitantly towards it and observed its inscriptions. Unintentionally overlooking its smaller markings my eyes wandered to the spear's centre. I looked at the bold letters placed purposefully in the middle. The words read "Creative Miracles".

Now, when I came out of this encounter I was extremely excited because after you experience something like that you know that God is going to show up in power. I arrived at the church two days later and started speaking out the words of knowledge that the Lord gave me. One by one the people were called out and healed. The woman who had the lump under her rib cage was healed that night, and the man's hip received healing. God was moving in power! There was a woman whose rib cage was cracked out of place, after I declared healing over her I asked her to do something that she couldn't do before. She told me that because her rib cage was out of place she couldn't do sit-ups, so she got down and started trying. On her second sit-up you could actually hear her rib cage crack into place audibly and she was healed.

While I was speaking I mentioned the encounter that I had in heaven a few days earlier but forgot to mention the lightning bolts that were around the spear. While I was going around praying for people there was a woman standing at the other side of the church worshipping. No one was even praying for her, but when she opened her eyes she saw with her natural eyes a lightning bolt shoot out of heaven, come into the church and it hit her right in the forehead! This woman was knocked onto the ground and she started convulsing in an encounter with Jesus that lasted about 45 minutes. After her encounter she got up and was healed from a constant migraine that she had for five months. Praise God!

Isn't this exciting? Literal perfection is in hand's grasp. I just got excited even writing that. I'll share another testimony with you to fan the fire that's starting to turn inside of you. A few years ago a friend and I were at a bus station on our way downtown in Ottawa, Ontario. We were only talking for a couple of minutes when a man who was drunk walked up to us. We introduced ourselves and in turn got his name. We hung out with our new friend Kevin for a while just having fun and telling jokes.

At this point I had a revelation of the kingdom for some time so I asked him, "Kevin, do you want to be completely delivered of your alcohol addiction right now?"

I think he got the idea that we were Christians because he started fumbling his words trying to come up with an answer, when suddenly his bus pulled up right in front of us giving him the chance for a quick escape. He leaped at the excuse and hopped on the bus without saying a word to us.

We could have let him go, but we thought this guy was awesome and we just loved him way too much, so we got on the bus with him. He was sitting at the back with another man who seemed to be a friend that he had just bumped into. Looking up, he caught my eye and looked down immediately, clearly trying to avoid us. When we made our way to the back of the bus we sat directly across from him. As I began to talk to him I had to push down a laugh because I thought the whole scenario was hilarious.

I said to him "Kevin, if you let me pray for you right now, God is going to get rid of your addiction completely."

This time he had nowhere to run so he threw up his hands saying "Fine! Just go for it!"

I laid my hand on his shoulder and declared, "Jesus, I release your kingdom over this man and I declare that he is sober."

God's presence slammed down on us. The man sobered up instantly to the point where we couldn't even smell the slightest bit of alcohol on him anymore. He felt God's presence so strongly that he was actually frozen still, unable to move or talk. We stayed and spent some more time sharing God's love with him. Another son was born into God's kingdom.

Two months later I bumped into Kevin's friend who he sat down with on the bus that day. He told me that not only was Kevin completely delivered from his addiction, but that he himself also received deliverance from his own alcohol addiction when God's presence fell in the bus!

See, these are a couple of examples to give us an understanding of what happens when the kingdom of heaven invades earth. The supernatural happens because a supernatural realm invades the natural. Sickness and pain have to leave because light drives out darkness. Insecurities, addictions and fears are dethroned because truth is the highest authority. This was Jesus' mandate in coming to earth. He came as a pioneer to establish the culture of the kingdom of heaven, which outweighs the world's culture that says bondage is to be tolerated. By making the kingdom attainable, as the King of kings Jesus brought forth true justice by putting an end to the enemy and his schemes.

"Power at its best is love implementing the demands of justice, and justice at its best is love correcting everything which stands against love."

- Dr. Martin Luther King, Jr.

The First Reigning King And Queen

To gain an understanding of man's relationship with God's kingdom we are going to briefly examine Adam and Eve's early life from when they lived in the garden.

In the beginning God created the earth, and on the earth in Eden He planted a garden. *Eden* in the Hebrew tongue is translated 'place of pleasure'. The garden was a place where heaven and earth overlapped one another. The garden was literally a habitation place for the kingdom of heaven. Heaven didn't just manifest in the garden on special occasions, the garden was heaven's dwelling place to rest. God's kingdom had full reign. When He created Adam and Eve to live in the garden they both lived in perfect love, perfect health, peace, joy and abundant blessing. They suffered from no ailments because sickness didn't exist in this garden.

Adam and Eve were flawless. Heaven's principles were all in fruition and a culture of perfection was in effect.

Genesis 1:26-27; "God said, 'Let Us make man in Our image, according to Our likeness; let them have dominion over the fish of the sea, the birds of the air, and over the cattle, over all the earth and over every creeping thing that creeps on the earth.' So God created man in His own image; in the image of God He created him; male and female He created them."

When God said this, He was saying that He was going to create man and woman to have dominion to rule and reign not only over the garden where heaven and earth dwelt together, but also over the whole earth in relationship with God. God made them the highest authority in heaven and earth under Himself. Adam and Eve could command the animals and they would have to listen. They could order a fig tree to wither and it would. If all creation was under submission to man, they could even speak to a mountain and command it to be thrown into the sea and it would obey. Just as any governing authority, whatever they spoke forth in the land that was given to them was established.

I feel a great importance to emphasize that contrary to what many people believe, Eve was actually called to co-reign along side of Adam. Eve's name means 'life' because she was the mother of all living (Genesis 3:20). If you go on to read Genesis 1:28 it says; "Then God blessed them, and God said to them,

'Be fruitful and multiply; fill the earth and subdue it;have dominion over the fish of the sea, over the birds of the air, and over every living thing that moves on the earth.'" People often only assume Adam's position of royalty because two verses earlier God directs this same authority only to 'man'. However, in verse 28 God clearly says that this authority is for both man and woman. This shows us that in this context when God says 'man' He is referring to mankind which includes woman. Needless to say, if you notice me mentioning 'man' in more of a general sense know that I'm referring to mankind.

Adam and Eve were first called to steward the garden where the kingdom had complete reign. Adam would tend the garden to keep it in check and order, maintaining it as a proper partner for the kingdom of heaven to be bound to. After learning to steward the garden with wisdom and integrity, eventually they would be ready to complete their mandate to "be fruitful and multiply, to fill the earth and subdue it" (Genesis 1:28). When God gave Adam and Eve this mandate it was as if He was saying, "Be faithful in tending and taking care of the garden because I have given you authority and dominion not only in Eden, I have also called you to expand beyond the garden to rule and reign over all of the land of the earth. So be fruitful and multiply the kingdom atmosphere that is in the garden beyond the garden. In doing this eventually there won't just be one garden that's a habitation place of the kingdom of heaven, but the whole earth will be the habitation place." Many of us think that Adam and Eve were just restricted to the garden, when really their kingdom mandate was to expand beyond it to the nations. If they had fulfilled this, man would have walked in his inheritance to reign in the nations since the beginning of time. The fullness of all government would have been upon the shoulder of the son.

When Adam and Eve made the decision to eat from the tree of the knowledge of good and evil, their punishment wasn't just to be taken out from the garden where heaven and earth co-existed as one. They were in actuality taking a step down from their position as king and queen over the nations. Adam and Eve abandoned their crowns, disinheriting mankind from their rightful place of royalty for the next thousands of years. The government that once rested upon the shoulder of man was delivered to the shoulder of the enemy.

Luke 4:5-6 says; "Then the devil, taking Him up on a high mountain, showed Him all the kingdoms of the world in a moment of time. And the devil said to Him, 'All this authority I will give you, and their glory, for this has been delivered to me, and I give it to whomever I wish.'"

The garden was barricaded from the rest of the world, therefore imprisoning the kingdom. From this point on man had to live a life outside of heaven's principles. Since governmental authority was passed from man to Satan, all of creation came under the tyranny of the enemy's iron rule. The kingdom of darkness began to take reign in man's heart making him vulnerable to sickness, pain, depression, fear of rejection and every other type of ungodly stronghold which lasted for thousands of years. The kingdom of heaven's principles were forgotten and a new law of unavoidable bondage was set in place.

This historical account recorded in scripture is the skeleton of every good medieval and fantasy tale. Creation and mankind remained crushed under dark rule waiting for a great hero to be born. Waiting for an heir to the throne to rise to take His rightful crown. One who would be the salvation of all mankind, restoring what was lost from the beginning and destroying the enemy and his works.

All Government Upon The Shoulder Of The Son

Isaiah 9:6-7; "For unto us a Child is born, Unto us a Son is given; And the government will be upon His shoulder. And His name will be called Wonderful, Counselor, Mighty God, Everlasting Father, Prince of Peace. Of the increase of His government and peace there will be no end, Upon the throne of David and over His kingdom, to order it and establish it with judgement and justice from that time forward, even forever. The zeal of the Lord of hosts will perform this."

Adam and Jesus were both given from the Father a garden to tend and take care of. Both of them were given a garden where heaven and earth overlapped. However, where Adam had a garden that was external to him in Eden, Jesus Himself was the garden where heaven and earth dwelt as one. Jesus' body was the habitation place of God. The kingdom that was once restricted from mankind was reborn within the Son Jesus. The place of pleasure that Adam and Eve had lived in was now Jesus' internal reality.

John 1:51; "He said to him, 'most assuredly, I say to you, hereafter you shall see heaven open, and the angels of God ascending and descending upon the Son of Man.'"

Just as Adam tended a garden where the kingdom of heaven had complete reign, Jesus also had to allow the kingdom to have complete reign within Himself. Jesus being the King of the kingdom of heaven had to properly steward the garden so that He could complete Adam's mandate by eventually expanding the kingdom beyond the garden of self, to fill the earth and subdue it with God's order. This is why Jesus was called the last Adam (1 Corinthians 15:45). Jesus was the last Adam because He succeeded in the mandate which Adam failed.

Since we are made co-heirs with Christ (Romans 8:17), we get to partner in the full inheritance that Jesus received from the Father. Not only do we come and live under the principals of the kingdom of heaven, but we also reign as kings and queens with Jesus in His kingdom. This is why He is the King of kings. Every king and queen is given territory. Every king and queen is given land to reign in. Our job is to establish the reign of the kingdom of heaven in the land and territory that has been entrusted to us by the Father. When we do this with Jesus we are destroying the works of the enemy by bringing divine order.

Before we can come into a place where we are entrusted by God to steward the external land such as a community, a city or even the nations for the gospel to see kingdom advancement, we need to first come to a place of maturity where we can properly steward the internal land of one's self. Just as Jesus did we need to allow heaven's reign to consume us and have full dominion in the entirety of our being.

You are God's garden. You are His place of pleasure.

Revelation 1:6; "And (He) has made us kings and priests to His God and Father, to Him be glory and dominion forever and ever. Amen."

The Inner Land

The Complete Reformation

Acts 3:20-21; "And that He may send Jesus Christ, who was preached to you before, whom heaven must receive until the times of restoration of all things, which God has spoken by the mouth of all His holy prophets since the world began."

In order for us to receive heaven's reign in our being we first need to understand our identity as sons and daughters of God. In this verse we see that Jesus came to restore all things. If we want to understand our full identity that was taken back at the cross, we need to look back to the beginning when man was first created. The first thing that we are going to look at is Genesis 1:26. The entire purpose of creation was the Father's desire to find His Son on earth, so God spoke and said; "Let Us make man in Our image." This one statement goes much deeper than we think. Man was the only part of creation that was made in the image of God. It wasn't the animals or plants, it was man. Mankind was the only part of creation that was born in the same class as God.

Psalm 8:4-5 says; "What is man that you are mindful of him, And the son of man that you visit him, For You have made him a little lower than the angels."

The Hebrew word for 'angels' in this verse is *Elohim* which means 'God'. The same God who spoke the earth into existence, who created the planets, stars and galaxies created us in His image a little lower than Himself. Since we are created in the image of God, if we are to come to a complete understanding of who we are as sons and daughters we first need to see and know the Father who created us.

When Jesus walked the earth as a man He had an incredible understanding of His identity in the Father:

John 5:19-20; "Most assuredly, I say to you, the Son can do nothing of Himself, but what He sees the Father do; for whatever He does, the Son also does in like manner. For the Father loves the Son, and shows Him all things that He Himself does."

Perfect transparency and trust reigned between Jesus and the Father. Since the Father loved His Son, He showed Him all that He did. He hid nothing of Himself from His Son. Jesus the Son, for His part, hid nothing from His Father. He chose not to cover Himself with fig leaves to keep parts of Himself secret. The Son didn't see Himself, but instead kept His eyes on His Father. He knew the depths of His Father. Jesus didn't have to engage His own heart and soul to understand Himself. Instead He engaged His Dad's heart. Since the Son is made in the image of the Father, when Jesus understood the depths of His Father He understood the depths of Himself. This is the foundational revelation that shapes a complete son who knows his true identity. He finds himself in the Father.

This move of God that's taking place is about sons and daughters who know their Daddy God in an intimate relationship and who constantly live their lives from that place of love and acceptance from Him. The more that our focus is on the Father and Jesus the complete Son, the more Jesus the Son will be revealed and formed within us. Look at what the apostle Paul says in Galatians 4:19; "My little children, for whom I labor in birth again until Christ is formed in you." Paul's initial mandate as an apostle was to present every believer as complete in Christ, that Jesus would be formed in His fullness in every believer. As Jesus is formed within us the attributes of heaven begin to manifest and take shape in our lives.

In the North American church we have in many ways forgotten the internal work of formation. We have believed that if we have new programs and create a proper external structure that people would reach spiritual maturity by being in our manmade wineskin. However, this is not the way that Jesus brought forth true sons and disciples. Jesus built within a man. Jesus' disciples saw Him and in turn saw the Father. As they saw Christ and made Him their focus, Jesus began to be formed within them. We can't start with an external revival because the external is the by-product of first an internal revival. Remember what God said to Ezekiel in Ezekiel 3:10-11:

"Moreover he said to me: 'Son of man, *receive into your heart all My words that I speak to you*, and hear with your ears. And go, get to the captives, to the children of your people and speak to them and tell them, 'Thus says the Lord God,' whether they hear, or whether they refuse.'"

See, before Ezekiel could speak the word of the Lord to the Israelites he was commanded to first receive the word in his own heart. When he first had a personal revelation of God's word for the Israelites, it could be spoken with authority. Jesus said that what we have freely received we should freely give away (Matthew 10:8), meaning that we can't give away what we haven't already received ourselves. As kings and queens we can't come into a place of maturity to properly present Jesus to the nations until Jesus the Son is first formed within us.

Exodus 33 talks about how Moses and Joshua would spend time in the tent of meeting where the glory of the Lord dwelled. After time passed Moses would depart and attend to His ministry duties, whereas Joshua would remain in the tent spending time with the Lord. After Moses died and Joshua was called to lead the Israelites into the Promised Land, Joshua had an encounter with the Lord that transitioned Him into walking into his greater calling.

Joshua 5:13-15; "And it came to pass, when Joshua was by Jericho, that he lifted his eyes and looked, and behold, a Man stood opposite him with His sword drawn in His hand. And Joshua went to Him and said to Him, 'Are You for us or for our adversaries?' So He said, 'No, but as Commander of the army of the Lord I have now come.' And Joshua fell on his face to the earth and worshiped, and said to Him, 'what does my Lord say to His servant?' Then the Commander of the Lord's army said to Joshua, 'Take your sandal off your foot, for the place where you stand is holy.' So Joshua did so."

See, before Joshua could walk in his calling as a commander to lead Israel into the Promised Land, he needed to first know God the Leader and Commander. As Joshua began to see and know Him, God the Commander began to be formed within him. We are coming to a time in the church when leaders won't be recognized by their credentials. Pastors and teachers won't be known because of their degrees. We will know them because we see Jesus our Pastor and Teacher formed within them. We will know true kingdom businessmen, not based on their bank account balance, but because we see that Christ the Businessman has been built within them. Their calling and identity will be a direct result of spending time with the Lord. The reformation that started in the 1400's didn't start with the external culture of the church being transformed, it started when Christ was formed within the hearts of John Wycliffe, John Hus, and Martin Luther. We are still living in the times of reformation because Christ is still being formed within His people.

When Jesus walked the earth He said that "the foxes have holes and birds of the air have nests, but the Son of Man has nowhere to lay His head" (Matthew 8:20). Jesus now stands as the mature and complete head and is looking for a place to rest. He can't rest to have full headship and reign over the body (the church) if the body hasn't grown up yet into a mature and complete man. He also can't rest upon a thought-up structure that the body has attempted to build. As the body we need to move from a place of adolescence to a place of wholeness where we are willing to receive and properly steward Jesus' headship and leadership. The only way for the body to mature and grow up is for Jesus the Son to be formed within it. The Son needs to be built and established within the inner man of the church, allowing the kingdom to reign in full authority.

Receiving From A Place Of Rest

In the cool of the day Adam would walk with God in the garden. He walked in close relationship and intimacy with Him. Apart from intimacy with God we will never see heaven's full reign in our lives. This is the place where the formation of the Son starts. We neither see Him nor enter into close relationship with God by striving. We also don't need to minister out of a place of striving in our own strengths. We see Him and minister from a place of resting in Him. Even though Jesus had no place to rest His head in the natural realm, in the realm of the Spirit He could rest in the arms of the Father to constantly minister from that place of rest.

Throughout this book I'm going to share a few testimonies as a tool that will enable me to deposit understanding into you. I will share some stories of how God showed up and moved powerfully to encourage you. I will also share with you some of the mistakes I've made while learning how to walk in the revelation that I'm teaching. This way you can learn from my shortcomings and hopefully grow quicker than I myself did.

Several years ago before I was released into having any form of platform in ministry, I had a strong drive to see God show up in the streets through evangelism. I loved going out to see Jesus reveal Himself through miracles, signs, wonders, words of knowledge, you name it. I would be downtown or at the hospitals diligently stepping out in faith and taking risks.

One morning, I woke up with a sudden urge to go out and love on people downtown with Jesus. The anointing was crisp for miracles, almost irresistible. My head popped off my pillow and without thinking twice I was on my way out. While leaving my house, I was halfway through the door when the Lord spoke to me.

"Luc, where are you going?"

God didn't speak to me in a big scary booming voice. He instead spoke calm like a Teacher who was strategically setting me up for a lesson.

I replied; "Oh you know Lord, I'm just going to share Your love with a few people downtown."

"Ah, I see." The tone of His response told me that He was analyzing my answers to His questions. "And why is it that you're going?"

I felt a small smirk growing on my face. I sensed His test, but my overconfidence led me to misinterpret what He wanted to teach me. I didn't realize it at the time, but I was setting myself up for a good-old Fatherly correction.

In my blind zeal I fell right into His trap and responded; "God, you know why I'm going; I'm going out to tell people about your love!"

I thought that God was testing my passion when really He was highlighting to me my motives. Then His response came, side-swiping me off of my self-made pedestal and right onto my back, crushing my pride beneath me. He said to me; "How are you supposed to share My love with people if you still don't know how to receive it yourself?"

I was really taken aback by God's response and to be quite honest slightly offended. However, the rebuke proved to be beneficial because it provoked me to stay in that day to pray and examine my heart a little bit. Hesitant to receive this lesson, I quieted my thoughts and asked God to reveal to me what He had meant. He began to show me that although I had a deep love for Him, I was trying to receive His love out of a place of striving. I began to see that I had swallowed a lie. I made the mistake of believing that His acceptance of me depended on the number of good things I did. Every person that I prayed for on the streets and saw healed was just another notch on my belt to make me feel good about myself. My insecurity of not feeling accepted by the Father was my drive. Evangelism wasn't about the people and how much the Father loved them, it became about me. This was really when the realization sunk in that if I were ever to be part of a move of God, I first needed to see a move of God in my own heart. I needed to experience an internal revival.

God began to transition me into a season where He would have me step back from anything that would tempt me to strive to receive His love. He began to show me the depths of my own heart and started revealing to me the errors in my mindset and motives. Over time I started to see that I wasn't an orphan who had to fight for my Father's love and affection, but that I am a son who gets to rest in the fact that my Daddy God loves me. I took many months to soak in this new revelation of love and acceptance to allow this truth to sink deep.

My very DNA started to change as I began to feel my Father's heart toward me. I started to understand that He loves me unconditionally, that He is proud of me and that He delights in my very being. He isn't mad with me, sad or even disappointed. The truth of His word trumped the lies that I believed about myself for years. I no longer saw myself as unworthy; I no longer feared rejection by Him. I put my striving aside because I understood finally how to receive from a place of resting in Him. Instead of praying for hours hoping that God would notice me, in my mind's eye I would just sit with Him for hours crying on His shoulder, overwhelmed by the fact that He loves me just the way that I am. From this point on any type of ministry that I did was done with joy and ease. The results of God's power moving in people's lives through me increased tenfold because I wasn't ministering anymore with a hidden agenda. I could confidently and successfully reflect the love of my Father because I knew that I was the apple of His eye.

Jesus is the vine and we are the branch that produces fruit. The branch doesn't have to strive to produce fruit; it just sits and receives the sap. Since it receives from the vine, the fruit is great because the vine is great. The branch isn't in a state of striving but of simply being. The Father receives us just as we are. We don't have to strive to be accepted by Him. We also don't need to strive to do great things for Him, we just need to be. Our works will be great because He is our source. In the same way, a flower doesn't have to strive to receive light from the sun to be nourished and grow; it just receives and grows out of a place of rest because it's a flower's identity to receive from the sun to flourish and become beautiful. As sons and daughters of God we don't need to strive to receive Dad's love, we just receive it because it's our identity as children to be loved by Him.

As long as we are still striving to be accepted we are living under the mindset of the law. This is true in the sense that we believe our right standing with God is dependent on what we do instead of what Jesus has already done, which is pride at its finest. John the Baptist said in John 3:30; "He must increase and I must decrease." Notice how this doesn't say 'I must decrease and He must increase'. His increase has to come before our decrease, not vice versa. Sometimes we think that we need to fix ourselves up and do a few good acts before we can walk into the Holy of Holies, when all that we need to do is step into Him and experience His increase because in His glory our flesh and sin can't stand. What we focus on we empower, so if all I'm doing is focusing on myself and trying to eliminate my sin in my own strength, I can actually be empowering its activity in my life. Remember, you are created in the image of the all-powerful God; even the smallest thing you focus on, you give strength and life to. When we look at Jesus, we empower Him in our lives and we begin to forget about our shortcomings because His greatness is so captivating. In the Old Testament, God set the seventh day apart as a day of rest. The number seven in prophetic numerology is the number of completion. We know that Jesus died for a complete and everlasting rest. We no longer have to try to receive Him in our own strength, but instead we receive by grace.

The cross permitted us to be adopted into sonship, living a life of perfect standing in the sight of our Father.

Restlessness at times can be a symptom of someone who is looking for the Father's love but just doesn't know where to look. We try step-to-step formulas to try to be close to Him, but all that we need to do is rest in the revelation that He loves us. Intimacy with God is the thing that I hold closest to my heart. He is my best friend and the love of my life. Every stem of ministry needs to come out of this place with Him. One of the enemy's greatest tactics is to try to make a man or woman of God busy to force them to step out of the secret place. The quickest way to burn out is to try to walk in your anointing apart from the revelation of the Father's love. If we minister apart from this truth we will minister out of a place of striving which leads to exhaustion. When we strive we cut off our ability to receive, but still try to constantly pour out. Whereas if we minister out of intimacy and rest, everything that we do becomes an encounter with God. Close relationship expands beyond our one-on-one time with Him. Every word of knowledge or miracle that we speak or see becomes a profound encounter with Jesus, even though we are the ones who are speaking the words and laying hands on the sick. Every business sale becomes an encounter with God the Provider. Every conversation that we have with someone transforms us because we begin to see Jesus within the words and the people that we are speaking with. We come to a place where we see Him everywhere because we constantly fix our gaze on Him. As we go from glory to glory and experience to experience this revelation of full acceptance in Him begins to take reign in our lives. The time gaps between glories and experiences begin to shorten until we are living in a constant glory and a never ending love encounter with Him.

Shortly after I had received the revelation of walking in intimacy with God through rest I had an encounter with Him that put things into good perspective for me. One night I was lying on my bed talking with Holy Spirit. Mid-conversation with Him I began to have an encounter where my spirit left my body. In my spirit I could look down and see my body lying on my bed. I continued to ascend through my ceiling and into the sky until I had left the earth completely. I was eventually hovering in front of the sun admiring its enormity. The heat that penetrated off of the big ball of flame felt excruciatingly wonderful. God's voice cracked like thunder from the sun allowing the vibration of His words to echo deep within my being.

He said to me, "I give you the same opportunity as I have given all of the others. You can come as close to the Son as you want. Although, far too often people take their eyes off of the Son and look back to the world. The closer you come to Me, the more that the flames will burn within you. As the flames burn, your desire to look back at the world will cease to exist."

After soaking in the sun's heat for a time, Holy Spirit prompted me away to journey through the galaxy with Him. Since God's word had pierced me to the core, I was more internally focused instead of externally aware of what was around me even in my current surroundings. As incredible as the galaxy looked; to be honest, I was just relieved to have some time to meditate on what God had just spoken into my life. Still wanting more time to soak in God's words, I found myself hovering before a black hole somewhere in the universe.

The same voice that spoke through the sun broke forth in power through the black hole. God spoke saying, "I give you the same opportunity as I have given all of the others. These are the deep secrets of My heart. If you pursue My heart and receive My love then you can have access to all of them. Although, far too often men fear the truth so they choose not to know."

I felt my emotions swelling with sadness when God told me He desired for everyone to know the deep secrets of His heart, but that they were seldom sought after. I closed my eyes trying to barricade my tears from escaping. Suddenly, the atmosphere shifted. My rapidly-running mind eventually discovered that my spirit had come back to earth and into my body. I laid in bed contemplating what I had just witnessed and heard. While relaxing in the comfort of God's presence I started to feel something like pins and needles prickling my face. I tried to avoid the feeling so that I could rest, but curiosity already had its hook in me. Feeling slightly disoriented, I got up and went to go look in the mirror to see what was wrong. When I stared at my reflection in the mirror, I realized that even though it was the middle of winter, my face was completely sunburnt after being so close to the sun in my encounter.

Resting In God's Presence

1 Samuel 3:3-4; "And before the lamp of God went out in the tabernacle of the Lord where the ark of God was, and while Samuel was lying down, that the Lord called Samuel. And he answered, "Here I am!"

Samuel's act of sleeping by the ark of God was a prophetic foreshadow of how through the cross we get to experience God's presence from a place of rest. One of the beautiful mysteries of heaven is that we are all God's best friend. He enjoys us so much that He wants to spend all of His time with us. This is why He will never leave us nor forsake us. We don't have to convince Him to hang out with us because His presence is always at hand. There was a Christian monk who lived in the 1600's whose name was Brother Lawrence. Brother Lawrence came to a revelation that God always wanted to fellowship with him to the point where he was constantly in an experiential state with Jesus. He never left the place of intimacy. People would actually come from across the world to watch this man do the dishes because everyone who came around him would feel and sometimes even see the presence of God glowing from him.

I am going to give you a quick exercise to help demystify our accessibility to experiencing God's presence:

Ok, I'm going to get you to close your eyes and clear your head. Now when you're ready I want you to start thinking about your favourite type of food. Meditate on how good it would taste if you were eating it right now. Do this for about 30 seconds.

Now, I want you to begin to meditate on how much God loves you. About how happy He is with you because you are His son or daughter. Do this again for about 30 seconds.

When you shifted your thoughts from food to God's love, did you feel a difference at all? How did you feel emotionally? Did you feel more loved? Did you feel happy or more at peace? If so, then you just experienced God's presence. See, you don't have to fast for 20 days and then pray for eight hours to get a glimpse of God's goodness, because we always have access to experience God in His presence. In order for us to live in a constant encounter with the God of love, all that we need to do is acknowledge His awareness by faith. It's in this place of relationship that we are transformed. For this reason, we need to make the choice to practise His presence whether we are at home praying, in the shopping mall with our family, or at the office working. It's an incredible thought to know that we have a best friend who has committed to never leaving our side. Even if we are working through issues, if we are having a bad day, or trying to constantly turn our backs on Him, God is completely committed to being in relationship with us.

God desires to be so deeply intimate with us. He wants us to come to Him as sons and daughters to be loved on by Him in spite of our shortcomings. Jesus' disciple John had a profound revelation that He was received by Jesus just the way that he was. In the gospels it isn't hard to see that the disciples needed some character growth. They were in constant competition with one another and their zeal far outweighed their wisdom. In spite of this, look at how John relates with Jesus;

John 13:23-26 says; "Now there was leaning on Jesus' bosom one of His disciples, whom Jesus loved (John). Simon Peter therefore motioned to him to ask who it was of whom He spoke. Then, leaning back on Jesus' breast, he said to Him, 'Lord, who is it?' Jesus answered, 'It is he to whom I shall give a piece of bread when I have dipped it.' And having dipped the bread, He gave it to Judas Iscariot, the son of Simon."

I don't believe that Jesus walked in this close of a relationship with John because He favoured John. I believe all of the disciples had the choice to be so close to Jesus where they could intimately lay their heads on Jesus' chest to ask Him secrets. John just made the decision to walk out the revelation in knowing that Jesus desired a deep love relationship with him. John being the author of this gospel even calls himself "the one whom Jesus loved" (John 21:20). He didn't write this out of pride, but was simply stating truth because he had a deep revelation that Jesus loved him just the way that he was. John didn't have to wait until he walked in

45

complete maturity before he could know Jesus like this, it was knowing Jesus like this that made him mature. Since John knew that Jesus adored him, he had the confidence to ask Jesus secrets and expect an answer back. This is probably why God trusted John to receive the important and heavenly secrets that were recorded in the book of Revelation.

Notice how Peter had prompted John to ask Jesus who would betray Him instead of asking Him himself. This implies Peter actually thought that John had a better chance receiving the answer than he himself did. In reality Peter could have walked in the same level of intimacy as John did, but instead feared that he would be turned away. I point that out to say this: you are not considered second best to God your Father and He doesn't prefer others above you. You are the apple of His eye and His delight is in your very being. Not only does He love you but He actually genuinely likes you as a person. Take advantage of this revelation. Your Father in heaven loves you just the way that you are. You are His beloved son or daughter and you can boldly approach His throne whenever you please. Even if you have no place to rest your head in the natural, you can rest your head between your Daddy's shoulders in the heavenly realms just like John did with Jesus.

Deuteronomy 33:12; "Of Benjamin he said: "The beloved of the LORD shall dwell in safety by Him, Who shelters him all the day long; And he shall dwell between His shoulders.""

You are highly blessed and favoured. Your Daddy God is proud of you. You are His delight. He loves you just the way you are. He believes in your dreams. You are so beautiful to Him. You are brilliant. You are so precious, so priceless, so loved.

Man's Three-Fold Being

1 Thessalonians 5:23; "Now may the God of peace Himself sanctify you completely; and may your whole spirit, soul, and body be preserved blameless at the coming of our Lord Jesus Christ."

If we are going to experience the Father's love for us and experience an internal revival, it's important to understand the different areas of our being where we receive Him. We know that God Himself is a Trinity. He is God the Father, God the Son Jesus, and God the Holy Spirit. He is three in one. Since we as men and women are created in His image, we need to understand that we were also created as a trinity. We are three men in one. We are born of body (the natural man who has five natural senses - in the Greek *soma*), soul (our heart which is the seat of our emotions - in the Greek *psyche*) and spirit (our mind and the spiritual man who has five spiritual senses - in the Greek *pneuma*). Those who think that the Trinitarian belief is hard to understand can learn from this way of thinking. I understand that the whole concept of three in one is hard to wrap our heads around at times, but when we take into consideration that we were created in the same model it simplifies matters greatly.

With my body I can be mowing the lawn, while with my soul I can be experiencing happiness, and with my spirit I can be praying in tongues or focusing on God. We live a life doing three different things all at once unaware that we are even doing it. We function as a trinity with ease because we were created to do so. If we can operate daily as a complete three-fold being then God is more than capable of doing the same, considering that the blueprint of our image was modelled directly from His own. In the same way that we are made of body, soul and spirit, Jesus plays the role of the 'body', the Father functions as the 'soul' and Holy Spirit stands in the role of 'spirit'. As three-fold beings we are formed and fashioned in His image, bearing His very likeness.

When God gave Moses the design of the temple that would be the habitation place of God's glory, He gave very detailed instructions saying "See that you make it according to the pattern shown you on the mountain" (Exodus 25:40). The writer of Hebrews elaborates by telling us that the pattern given to Moses was a pattern of the tabernacle in heaven (Hebrews 8:5). I believe that the pattern of the temple that Moses copied in heaven was in fact Jesus, since Jesus' body was the first human temple to inhabit the glory of God.

When Jesus died, the temple that was made of stones was destroyed as a prophetic declaration that the glory of God would no longer reside in a temple made by man, but that man himself would be the temple. The design of the temple that Moses received from God had four main sections; it had the outer court which led to the inner court. After crossing the inner court you would enter the Holy place which finally led to the Holy of Holies. Since the first temple was a prophetic foreshadow of Jesus the temple, we need to understand their parallel to understand our three-fold being. Our body is the outer court that encases our entire being; it is the face of the temple. Our soul is the inner court. After the soul is the Holy place which is our spirit and then finally the Holy of Holies which is the kingdom of heaven, God's dwelling place (Luke 17:21). We need to allow the kingdom to move outward past the Holy of Holies to also reign in the Holy place. From there it will continue outward to the inner court, then past the outer court and beyond it to the world.

1 Peter 2:5; "You also, as living stones, are being built up a spiritual house, a holy priesthood."

The Adamic Race

Earlier we took a look at what happened after the fall of man and its governmental effects. Now, we are going to observe its direct effect on man's personal identity. While Adam and Eve still lived in the garden they lived a life where they were both fully mature in their three-fold being. They were flawless in body, soul and spirit, bearing the unveiled image of God. When Adam and Eve ate from the tree of the knowledge of good and evil they literally gave up their right to walk in their complete identity as a son and daughter of God. The wholeness that they experienced within themselves was compromised. Once they were banned from the garden and sin began to take reign in them, everyone who was born into this world after Adam and Eve were born into a lineage of death.

The origin of heaven and hell (sin) are in every man and woman, just as the tree of life and the tree of the knowledge of good and evil are in the garden. I say this in the sense that the choice to come in alignment with heaven or sin is made within every person. As mankind continued to eat from the tree of the knowledge of good and evil from within himself, the foundation of hell and death began to be established in man's heart. Since this was the case, death began to eat at man from the inside out. Man gave the kingdom of darkness reign in his very core instead of heaven, giving hell authority to spread outwards. Since the spirit is the inner core of every person, death's plague first started there. So, as man continued to eat from the tree of the knowledge of good and evil we began to lose understanding of our spiritual identity. Death began to kill our spirit, leaving it lifeless and void. From this point on we no longer lived as a trinity but instead as two-fold beings, only operating in body and soul.

When our spiritual senses fell asleep we could no longer understand spiritual things. We forgot the wisdom of heaven and began to instead rely on man's wisdom which defiled our souls. Death quickly corrupted man's soul by filling his mind with worldly ideologies and philosophies which drove us to act out of a mindset of carnality. This is where emotional and mental bondages came into play. The fruit from the tree swept beyond the inner court into man's outer court which was his body. All sorts of sickness, disease and bodily disorders stepped into a place of authority over the body of man. As our hearts grew colder and we became more prone to violence, there eventually had to be a restriction placed upon our age, and man's lifespan was limited. Our once flawless image became deformed in contrast to its intended state, separating us from having any likeness to the eternal God.

Sounds pretty bad eh? It's a scary thought to think that death had this type of dominion over mankind, to the extent that we had completely forgotten who we were created to be. The word 'dominion' literally means 'to dominate'. Throughout the Old Testament, the kingdom of darkness dominated mankind into submission. We were a fallen race, living in the consequences of our disobedience.

Experiencing God In Our Three-Fold Being

Jesus was the perfect example of someone who saw and experienced the Father in His fullness. He was given the same choice as every man and woman that had gone before Him. He could either eat from the tree of life, or the tree of the knowledge of good and evil. Choosing life that His Father offered Him, Jesus lived apart from sin, giving the kingdom of darkness no foothold or place to have reign within Him. Instead of allowing hell to be established, He came into alignment with heaven permitting His Father's love to consume Him in wholeness. Jesus lived in perfect standing with the Father, which allowed Him to walk in the full inheritance of a Son. He could bask in the ecstasy of His Father's love in His entire being: in body, soul, and spirit.

The act of the cross allowed the complete inheritance of life and love to spill forth to anyone who would know Jesus as Saviour. The words 'to save' are translated from the Greek word *sozo* which means 'to make whole'. When we say that Jesus came to save us we are saying that He in fact came to make us whole. This means that no part of us has been left unfinished. We are 100% restored. Through the cross we have received His full salvation for our spirits, His full deliverance for our souls and His full healing for our bodies. Jesus came to save and restore the whole person that we would be presented as complete in Him. We get the awesome privilege of encountering the love of God not just in part, but in totality.

We are so blessed to have such a tangible and loving God. We are the apple of His eye and it is His good pleasure to encounter us with His love in the entirety of our very being! For so long in the North American church we have substituted encounters and revelation for an intellectual knowledge of Him. We need to have a love and hunger for knowledge, but we need to have more of a love and hunger for encountering Him. Paul said that, "Knowledge puffs up, but love builds up" (1 Corinthians 8:1). If we only have knowledge we will become puffed up, which means 'to be arrogant'. We need to be built up with love, and love is an experience! Memorizing scripture is the by product of encountering and experiencing Jesus through the Word of God. His Word is not a dead Word. It is living and active, sharper than any double-edged sword. Every verse and word in the Bible is God-breathed and is an open heaven for us to come into a revelatory encounter with Jesus. Psalm 34:8 says; "Oh, taste and see that the Lord is good." To taste and see is to experience. It's time that we make the choice to walk in the fullness of our inheritance which is Him.

As Christians we are supposed to set the example for every culture with the culture of the kingdom. How are we supposed to set an example for the drug culture unless we can show them that love encounters with Jesus are better than drug trips? We don't have to go to clubs or bars on Saturday nights to have a good time, we can drink of the new wine and be filled with His Spirit! We don't have to do drugs to feel intoxicated. We can be like the priests of the Old Testament who would be doing their priestly duties when the glory of God would come like a cloud to fill the temple. The priests would inhale and exhale the glory cloud to the point where they couldn't even stand anymore (2 Chronicles 5:13-14). God is looking for a people who won't be satisfied in just knowing about Him, He is looking for sons and daughters who will be in an intimate experiential relationship with Him.

We are going to take a look at each of the three parts of our being individually. We are going to learn about each of their functions in helping us operate, but we are also going to take a look at how we can learn to encounter God in each area. If I only tell you about them then you will only have knowledge of them, but if I teach you how to encounter God's love in each part then you will truly be transformed.

The Spirit Man

The first part of man's three-fold being that we are going to look at is the spirit man. Remember how man was created in the beginning. In the process of Adam's birth, God first took dust of the earth which was of the natural realm and formed Adam from it. Now in that moment Adam was given five natural senses to experience God through the natural realm around Him. He was given natural senses to see, hear, touch, taste and smell. After this in Genesis 2:7; God breathes into Adam the breath of life which is spirit. In that moment Adam was also given five spiritual senses to experience God in the spiritual realm around Him. Adam lived in two realms at the exact same time being in a constant awareness of his natural and heavenly surroundings. Adam's spiritual ears to hear were just as mature as his natural ears to hear. His spiritual eyes to see were just as mature as his natural sight. Just as he could see birds and trees, he could also see God and the angels. His day-to-day life consisted of tasting and seeing heaven.

We discussed before about how, after the fall of man, mankind had lost understanding of their spiritual identity. So, after Garden of Eden times man no longer had much of a grid for spiritual things. This is why God had to raise up prophets in the Old Testament, because mankind could no longer discern anything spiritual so therefore couldn't discern God's voice. This is also why such extreme measures were taken when a prophet was wrong in prophesying. Prophets of the Old Covenant had incredible influence to do things such as counselling kings and declaring strategy for war. They were God's mouthpiece on earth. So since a prophet had such high platform, if his prophetic word was wrong he would have to be put to death, because the others couldn't discern whether the rest of his words would be true or not. In the Old Testament, Holy Spirit would hover above the waters (Genesis 1:2) and when God the Father had a word that He wanted to speak to man He would speak the word to Holy Spirit. The Spirit of God would then come to the prophets and speak the word. Even the prophets didn't have spirits that were living and active, nor did they have Holy Spirit abiding in them. Holy Spirit at times would fill a person to empower them to do something, but He did not live in man in the Old Testament. This is why David said in the Psalms "Take not thy Holy Spirit from me" (Psalm 51:11). This is also why Isaiah's prophecy in Isaiah 11:2 was so profound when he said "The Spirit of the Lord shall rest upon Him." Isaiah was declaring that a Messiah was coming to earth and that the Spirit of God wouldn't just ascend and descend upon Him, but would actually rest and remain. Isaiah was prophesying of spiritual identity being restored.

Look at the parallel in how Adam and Jesus were created. Just as God took something of the natural (dust of the earth), and something from heaven (the breathe of life) to create Adam; in the same way God took Mary who was of the natural realm and the Spirit of the Lord came over her, the power of the most high overshadowed her (Luke 1:35). In that moment the spiritual seed of heaven came together with the natural egg of Mary and Jesus was conceived. See, Jesus was the second man in all of history to be born not only as a natural man, but also as one who understood His full potential as a spiritual man. Just as Adam before his fall could taste and see the Father with his spiritual senses, so could Jesus. Since Jesus is the last Adam and completed His mandate; now when we receive Holy Spirit, the pure Spirit of Christ comes and becomes one with our lifeless spirit. We become born of the Spirit and are given five spiritual senses to engage the Father and to experience heaven. We literally become new creations adopted into a heavenly and supernatural lineage.

In John 3, Jesus gave a brilliant teaching to a man named Nicodemus who was a Pharisee. What Jesus said in verse five is profound; "Most assuredly, I say to you, unless one is born of water and Spirit, he cannot see the kingdom of God." In this verse Jesus was talking about receiving the baptism of water and of the Holy Ghost, but I believe that this was also a teaching about identity. Read it again with me, "Most assuredly, I say to you, unless one is born of water (born of the natural realm) and Spirit (born of the spiritual seed of heaven), he cannot 'see' the kingdom of God." You are not just born as a natural being, but also as a spiritual being.

Unless I understand who I am and learn how to activate my spirit man's senses, I can't 'see' and experience the kingdom. We have five spiritual senses that need to be activated if we want to experience the fullness of God and heaven.

The supernatural has been very suppressed in the North American church. A lot of it is still considered along the new age way of thinking. When in reality, supernatural and spiritual experiences didn't start with the new age movement. Satan isn't the Creator so therefore he can't create, he can only pervert what God has already made. The supernatural is a way for believers to be in a relational experience with their God and it should be a constant and normal thing because we are supernatural in our DNA as Christians. Since we are born of the Spirit we have been given full access to experience heaven.

In 2 Corinthians 12:1-4 it says; "It is doubtless not profitable for me to boast. I will come to visions and revelations of the Lord: I know a man in Christ who fourteen years ago – whether in the body I do not know, or whether out of the body I do not know, God knows – such a one was caught up to the third heaven. And I know such a man – whether in the body or out of the body I do not know, God knows – how he was caught up into paradise and heard inexpressible words, which is not lawful for a man to utter."

Paul in his letter to the Corinthians mentions that he once knew a man who was caught up into the third heaven. Now, if there is a third heaven, then we need to assume that there is a first and second heaven also. Before God taught me to use my imagination, I imagined heaven to be a small place maybe as big as a city or MAYBE even a small country. But, I have learned that heaven is a wonderfully vast place. The first verse of the Bible, Genesis 1:1 says; "In the beginning God created the heavens and the earth." Notice how the word 'heavens' in this verse is plural where 'earth' is not. Even the size of earth can't compare to heaven's enormity. While we are talking about activating our spiritual senses, I am going to provide definitions and give testimonies about a few of the different realms of the heavens to bring clarity to what we now know is our full inheritance and right to experience. I will start with the first heaven.

The First Heaven

Genesis 28:12; "Then he dreamed, and behold, a ladder was set up on the earth, and its top reached the heaven; and there the angels of God were ascending and descending on it."

Most theologians will agree that the first heaven is the solar system. If you look in the creation account in Genesis 1:7 it talks about something called a 'firmament' which God named 'Heaven'. In verses 14-19 it talks about how the firmament is where the sun, moon and stars are. God has created man with the desire to uncover mystery. I can't imagine God creating the earth and the universe without giving His children the ability to explore and discover His creation. I know that this might seem like a very controversial statement but I believe that it's possible to encounter God in the galaxy through prophetic experience. We say that heaven is our inheritance and the Bible clearly states that the firmament is a heavenly place so there must be truth to this. In fact I know many other prophetic leaders who experience these types of encounters with God on a regular basis. I shared an experience earlier in the section 'Receiving From A Place Of Rest' where I had an encounter where I was taken in the spirit into the universe. If you would like to reread it to gain some context on what I am teaching right now, it would be beneficial and would help you understand what I mean.

First-heaven encounters normally take place through what is called an out-of-body experience, or in some charismatic groups is called being translated in the spirit. Having an out-of-body experience or being translated is different than being transported. Being transported is when our whole body is supernaturally taken from one place to another, just like Phillip was in Acts 8:39-40. Being translated is where your spirit leaves your body and goes elsewhere. The term out-of-body experience has, like many other Holy Spirit led manifestations, been branded and perverted by witchcraft and the occult, when actually it's something that is completely scriptural.

In 2 Kings 5 it tells a story about a commander of an army named Naaman. Naaman was plagued with leprosy and sought out the prophet Elisha in Israel to see if God would heal his body through Elisha. When he found the prophet's home, Elisha sent out a servant to tell Naaman to dip in the Jordan River seven times and that he would come out from the river healed. Naaman did as he was told and was healed. Not only was he healed but his skin restored like the flesh of a little child. He came back to Elisha offering him payment for the healing, but Elisha refused and sent him on his way. Now, Elisha's servant Gehazi became greedy and chased after the commander telling him that his master had changed his mind so that he could take the gifts for himself.

Look at what happens now. After Gehazi goes and takes money and clothes from Naaman, he comes back and tries to tell his master Elisha that he never went to see him at all. In verse 26 Elisha responds to him by saying; "Did not my spirit go with you when the man turned back from his chariot to meet you?" This verse says that Elisha's spirit actually left his body and went before him to watch his servant Gehazi take money and clothes that weren't rightfully his. Paul says a similar thing in 1 Corinthians 5:3; Paul explains to the Corinthians that he is absent from them in body, but present in spirit. The spirit is an amazing part of our being. Since it is spirit it isn't bound by natural law, which is why it doesn't have to be confined to the body and can go forth beyond it.

We are coming to a place in the body of Christ where we are going to be able to walk in these types of manifestations of the Spirit without having to fear that we are crossing into the new age territory. The worry stops when we can commune with Holy Spirit and trust Him in how He wants to speak to and lead us. Although I don't necessarily recommend trying to practise having out-of-body experiences, I do support being open to them when Holy Spirit leads. These types of encounters can be very profound, but ONLY when they are completely led and inspired by Holy Spirit. When we know how He speaks we can come to a place of trusting His leading in experiences like this without questioning.

Just to bring some clarity: Holy Spirit isn't an "it" or a "thing"; He is a person and our friend who has proven Himself to be trusted. He is our Helper, Teacher and Comforter. He is the personality of the Godhead and His desire is to reveal to us the deep things of the heart of God.

1 Corinthians 2:10 says; "God has revealed them to us through His Spirit. For the Spirit searches all things, yes, the deep things of God. For what man knows the things of a man except the spirit of a man which is in him? Even so no one knows the things of God except the Spirit of God. Now we have received, not the spirit of the world, but the Spirit who is from God, that we might know the things that have been freely given to us by God."

When we first receive Holy Spirit, He merges with our spirit and we become one spirit with Him (1 Corinthians 6:17). Holy Spirit walks in perfect relationship with the Father and the Son. Since He is constantly in fellowship with them, He is continually searching out the deep things of God. Our spirits are one with Him, meaning that our spirits can constantly be keeping in step with Holy Spirit while He is searching out the deep secrets of God's heart. It's comforting to know that there's a part in all of us that is never willing to stop pushing to know the full magnitude of who God is. Revelation 4 talks about the four living creatures who worship the Lord day and night. They are able to operate without the need for sleep because they are spiritual beings and therefore don't require physical rest. An exciting truth is that all night long while our bodies are sleeping, our spirits are hungrily awake interacting with God and constantly receiving from Him.

Job 33:16-17; "In a dream, in a vision of the night, when sleep falls upon men, while slumbering on their beds, then He opens the ears of men, and seals their instruction."

The Second Heaven

The second heaven is what I believe the apostle Paul referred to in Ephesians 6:12; "For we do not wrestle against flesh and blood, but against principalities, against powers, against the rulers of the darkness of this age, against spiritual hosts of wickedness in the heavenly places."

Let's camp out on the topic of the second heaven for a little bit. This verse shows us that Paul the apostle considered the spiritual realm where angels and demons battle to be a part of heaven. A lot of us in the church still get freaked out when something like angels are even mentioned, when really they should be a very common thing to be experienced as our spiritual senses begin to mature. We don't worship angels or focus on them, but we need to acknowledge them because they are a part of God's kingdom and a part of the reality of heaven. If we believe in the restoration of all things then technically our spiritual eyes should be just as mature as our natural eyes, just as Adam's and Jesus' were. Seeing in the spirit realm isn't a spiritual gift and it's not just for the prophets, it is for every believer.

Remember the story of Peter's miraculous escape from jail (Acts 12). Peter leaves the jail and goes to the house where the other believers are praying for his escape. When he knocks on the door a young girl named Rhoda comes, hears his voice and runs to tell the others that Peter escaped. Now, notice the believer's response: they said to her, "You are beside yourself... It is his angel" and then they go back to praying for Peter's escape. Let me point something out here, they believe that this is a physical manifestation of an angel knocking at their door and talking to a young girl, and yet they brush it off flippantly as if it isn't even a big deal. This is how normal it was for the early church to experience God moving through angels. If something like this happened in most churches people would be flipping their lids! I wouldn't be surprised that if in some places it even caused conflict and separation. Hebrews 1:14 says that God uses angels as ministering spirits to minister to those who will inherit salvation. If the saints of old have died then who else will they minister to other then you and I?

In Matthew 4:11, after Jesus was tempted by Satan in the desert it says "then the devil left Him, and behold, angels came and ministered to Him." If Jesus the Messiah needed angels to minister to Him then we definitely need to be humble enough to receive their ministry.

One time, I remember lying in my bed waiting eagerly for sleep to take me. I was slowly drifting off when the Lord abruptly woke me. He said, "Luc, I want you to stay up tonight and study the entire book of Revelation word for word so that I can reveal secrets about heaven to you." When He said that, right away two emotions sparked and flared up within me. My first emotion was extreme excitement because I love it when God tells me secrets. My second emotion was concern since it was already 12:00am and I knew that reading Revelation word for word was going to take me longer than a few hours. I let out a sound that was neither a cheer nor a sigh. It was my attempt at creating a noise that represented both joy and exhaustion at the same time. God only knows if I was successful. I said to Him,

"Alright Lord, I'm going to need some help with this."
Right when I asked Him for help I looked up and saw
two angels walk into my bedroom. Both of the angels
stood about five feet tall and didn't look a year younger
than 80 years old. The two old scribes wore simple grey
robes and carried scrolls that flashed from gold to silver
in constant repetition. They gracefully approached me
on my bed and took a seat beside me opposite from the
other. Their countenance radiated eagerness which told
me that they were waiting on me to start reading. The
second I opened my Bible I fell into a deep trance (Acts
11:5). As I read Revelation the angels read from their
scrolls and whispered secrets about heaven into my
ears. This encounter lasted for about six hours until I
passed out at around 6:00am.

Another time, I was sitting in a Tim Horton's
reading with God. I knew that I had nothing to do for
the day so I started asking God what He had on His
agenda. He responded and said; "Before you go to bed
tonight you are going to meet someone who has pain in
their left knee, lay hands on their knee and it will be
healed." I took the word in faith and went about my day
keeping an eye open for this person.

After running a few errands I realized that I had
gone throughout my entire day without running into the
person who had the pain in their knee. I went home and
lied sleeplessly in my bed. Hours passed until at about
1:00am I received a text from one of my friends who
convinced me to come and grab a coffee since sleep
apparently wasn't an option. We met at the exact same
Tim Horton's that I was reading at earlier in the day. I
was enjoying my large double double when the Lord told

me to step outside. Excusing myself, I made my way outdoors to stand in the parking lot. Not even five minutes passed before a homeless man walked up to me asking me for some change. I gave him some money and asked him his name and how he ended up living on the streets. He told me that his name was James and began to tell me that he used to be a construction worker for the city. Then it came, he told me that 10 years ago he hurt his knee on a job site and he's been on the streets ever since.

I was starting to get excited because I knew that this guy was the person I was waiting to find all day.

I said to James, "You hurt your left knee didn't you?"

Looking sceptical He replied; "Yes, how did you know it was my left knee?"

I began to tell James that God told me I was going to meet a man who had problems in his left knee, and that if he let me lay my hands on it, his knee would be healed. I got on my knees in the parking lot and touched his knee and it completely reconstructed on the spot. James was floored!

Holy Spirit then spoke to me and said, "Anything that this man asks of Me right now he will receive."

I asked James - if he could have one thing in the world, what it would be. He told me that he had shaken off every addiction he'd ever had except that he had been addicted to smoking for 25 years. He said that he'd tried everything but couldn't quit and it was starting to eat away at his body. As he was about to light the last cigarette of his pack I told him that if he let me pray for him, his addiction would be broken. Before He lit up he let his arm drop, now holding his last cigarette at his side waiting for me to pray. I began to speak to the addiction telling it to leave and declaring that the kingdom would dethrone his dependency on nicotine.

As I was speaking I looked to the right of me and saw an angel crouched over, slowly walking towards James. I watched it curiously. The angel finally reached him, and when it did it casually lifted its arm up and flicked the cigarette right out of his hand! James' eyes grew wider then I've ever seen on a man.

"Did you just see that?!" James bellowed.

Laughter erupted from me and I told him that if he stepped on the cigarette, his addiction would be broken. James jumped up in the air and stomped down hard. Since the kingdom of God was reigning there in the Tim Horton's parking lot, God kept on moving. This man who just got rocked by experiencing the love of God started falling into visions and began prophesying over me very specific and timely words. Long story short, James had a wild encounter with Jesus and had his spiritual eyes open to what was happening in the second heaven.

Understand that I don't share testimonies to boast in my own encounters. I share testimonies because Revelation 19:10 says that "the testimony of Jesus is the spirit of prophecy" meaning that every time I testify as to what Jesus has done in my life, I am actually prophesying that you are going to experience the same thing. If I say that I have seen the sick healed then I'm saying that you will lay hands on people and see sickness flee. If I say that I've seen angels, then I'm declaring that you will see them too. As I've said earlier, this next move of the Spirit that is about to take place globally isn't about a one-man-show, it's about every believer walking in the fullness of who they are in Christ. We need to get out of the mindset that these things are only for the few. You are wonderfully and supernaturally made.

Activating your spiritual senses has a lot to do with how observant you're willing to be. Often our eyes are so internally focused on our thoughts that we are completely unaware of what is happening around us. When you live life day-to-day, there are things constantly happening around you in the second heaven. The truth of the matter is that it's just as real as the natural realm. Next time you're in a church service take note of what you begin to feel spiritually when God is doing different things in the meeting. You will notice that things feel different in your spirit when the worship is happening compared to when the Word is being taught during a message. When God is moving in miracles in a service it feels different in the atmosphere compared to if there's a grace to give prophetic words because the anointing is different. It's important for us to develop an awareness of what's going on in heaven's atmosphere because it gives us revelation of what God is doing and what He is wanting to accomplish.

Just because of who you are in Christ I can guarantee you that there are angels around you even right now. Remember, they are ministering spirits, sent to minister to those who will inherit salvation. If you're saved, then you have angels ministering to you whether you know it or not. I encourage you to test this out in faith; take some time to ask Holy Spirit to show you what's happening in the spiritual atmosphere right now around you. Ask Him right now where there are angels in the room that you're in and what they look like. Begin to ask God to open your spiritual eyes. If God shows you something with your natural eyes then that's great, but don't limit yourself by only expecting that He will show you something with your natural senses. He wants to activate your spiritual eyes as well - otherwise you're only walking in half of your potential to see. Don't let awkwardness or a fear of God not showing you anything hold you back. God's heart is for you to experience your inheritance as a spiritual person. He who has eyes let him see and he who has ears let him hear. It's time that we begin to allow understanding of who we actually are to sink in.

The Third Heaven

Before I get into the theology of our right to see and experience the third heaven I'm going to start off this section with a testimony:

A few years ago I was at church worshipping God with a group of friends when I was taken into an encounter. I was in heaven. At this point in my life whenever I was in an encounter where I could see heaven I would be guided around by the same two angels. The angel that walked with me on my right side's name was Daniel. He looked very simple in appearance wearing a plain white robe. While his demeanour displayed modesty, his presence beamed nobility and integrity. On my left stood an angel whose face I could never see, no matter how hard I tried. I would always try to look, but my vision would instantly distort refusing me clarity. The two angels led me to walk down a road that looked as though it was made of stone. The street wasn't supported on solid ground, but instead stretched across heaven's sky. We walked for a time as the angel on my right pointed out different things I needed to see throughout heaven. A few hours passed when Holy Spirit drew my attention to the stone road that I was traveling. A sudden urge gripped me to lay my hand on the floor of heaven. I stopped mid-step, got down onto my knees and began brushing my hand across the rocky street. Wonder took me when I saw that I wasn't actually walking on a road made of stone, but that the grey stone look was actually dust covering the streets of gold. I stared in disbelief. The gold shone in absolute purity, mastered to perfection and incomparable to any type of metal that I had ever seen on earth.

Turning to the angel on my right I asked him why the streets were covered in dust. He spoke in a soft voice and said to me, "It is because not many people have walked where you are walking."

Holy Spirit then began to speak and said, "Even though not many people have walked where you're walking, I am about to release a revelation throughout the church where they will know and understand their access to the heavens. They will be able to touch the ground, they will be able to see the signs, and smell the fragrance of My presence."

Watching people getting activated to engage heaven is probably one of my favourite things to see in ministry. It is an incredible thing when sons and daughters begin to walk in the inheritance that has been theirs ever since they first received Jesus in their hearts. The third heaven is a dimension away from the first heaven and above the second heaven where angels and demons battle. It's the place in heaven where God's throne is, where the streets of gold are and where the mansions of the saints are. The third heaven is the place that is spoken about in chapters like Isaiah 6, Ezekiel 1 and Revelation 4.

I introduced a passage earlier (2 Corinthians 12:1-4) which mentions Paul talking about a man he once knew who, fourteen years ago, was caught up to the third heaven. Most theologians will agree that the man who Paul referred to in this verse was in fact himself and that he was using a writing style that was commonly used in those times and culture to humble the writer. I can only assume that since Paul would make radical statements such as Ephesians 1:3 where he says that "we are blessed with every spiritual blessing in the heavenly realms", that the theologians must have been right. I can't see him teaching something unless he had a true revelatory experience in that area.

Paul was such a radical teacher. Through his teachings he unveiled such weighty truths, such as how the gospel was to be accessible not only to the Jews but also to the Gentiles. He also brought forth the revelation that prophetic experiences weren't just for prophets anymore like they were in the Old Testament, but instead are for every believer. Look at what he says here in Ephesians 4:11-12; "He Himself gave some to be apostles, some prophets, some evangelists, some pastors and some teachers, for the equipping of the saints for the work of ministry, for the edifying of the body of Christ." Paul states here that a prophet's job in the church isn't just to be a mouthpiece for God, as it was before Jesus came to the earth. That is a piece of the call, but not all of it. He makes it clear that part of a prophet's function in the church is to train and equip others in the body to do what comes natural to a prophet. It is in a prophet's DNA to receive the word of the Lord and to encounter God in unusual ways through dreams, visions, trances, out-of-body experiences, angelic visitations, third-heaven encounters and countless other ways. He or she is a gift to the church, called to take what is a natural part of their DNA and make it a common part of the ENTIRE body of Christ's DNA. Paul radically walked out the revelation that whatever he could do in Christ, so could every man or woman. What a prophet or evangelist can do, so can every believer. It's a sobering thought to know that there aren't any lone ranger super heroes called to be the only ones who can engage heaven. We are all called to. We just first need wake up to believe that truth and then we can learn how to access what is already ours.

Look at what Jesus said in John 3:13; "No one has ascended into heaven but He who came down from heaven, that is, the Son of Man who is in heaven." (NKJV)

This verse may look like a brain teaser, but it's key to unlocking the mystery of our access to heaven. I would encourage you read it over a few times to really get it into your spirit.

Check out what Jesus said at the end of the verse, "WHO IS IN HEAVEN." Jesus was literally saying, Nicodemus, I'm here talking to you and sitting with you in the natural realm but I am also in heaven right now with My Father. Remember, Jesus constantly saw everything His Father did (John 5:19-20). Jesus was always in a love encounter with Daddy God, being completely saturated in experience with Him. He lived His life with one foot on the earth and one foot in heaven at all times. Since we are made co-heirs in Christ (Romans 8:17) this means that we get to partner in the full inheritance that Jesus received from the Father. So everything that Jesus walked in while He was on the earth, we also have the right to walk in. Jesus said that we would even do greater things. Just as Jesus walked both in heaven and on earth at the exact same time, we also walk in both realms. Paul said in Ephesians 2:6 that we are seated in heavenly places in Christ. This doesn't say that one day you will be seated in heaven; it says that you are there now! This isn't a philosophy or metaphor; this is your reality as a son or daughter of

God. Right now you are reading this book in the natural realm, but with your spirit you are in heaven.

In Ecclesiastes 1:14 Solomon says; "I have seen all the things that are done under the sun, all of them are meaningless, a chasing after the wind." Solomon was the most successful man who lived in the time before the cross. In his later years, he comes to the realization that everything is 'meaningless' and repeats the phrase "under the sun" 27 times.

Revelation 4:1 says; "After these things I looked, and behold, a door standing open in heaven. And the first voice which I heard was like a trumpet speaking with me, saying, 'Come up here, and I will show you things which must take place after this.'"

Today, because of what Christ has accomplished we have an open door to heaven and no longer have to live life "under the sun" - we can now live life 'above the sun'. Jesus is seated at God's right hand (Revelation 4:2) which means that His work is finished, so you have a blood-bought right and full access of all of heaven. In Christ all of heaven is yours.

I'm going to share another testimony with you to allow this truth to sink deeper. One time my friend Shawn and I were heading to a meeting that was geared towards soaking in God's presence. Previous to the soaking night I had taken a lot of time to soften him up to the idea that He could actually have a third-heaven encounter just like Paul did. This type of thinking was new to him so I encouraged him to be open minded to the possibility. When we got there, the soaking music turned on and we all started engaging God. I began to open my spiritual eyes to see what was going on in heaven. I was taken to a place that I had never been before. All around me I could see the vastness of the galaxy. Beneath my feet was what looked like a large sheet of glass in the shape of a diamond that stretched as far as about 200 feet. The crystal glass floor resembled a calm and steady lake that was resting underneath the starry sky. The floor was transparent which gave the illusion that it was just aimlessly floating through the universe. I could see that there was a door on one of the sides of the diamond platform which led to other parts of heaven.

For a time I thought that I was alone until I saw that there was a man standing on the glass platform who glowed like blue sapphire. I felt Holy Spirit speak to me, telling me that he was a saint who had passed and gone to heaven. I approached the saint sensing in my spirit that he had a message for me. His eyes were far away as he gazed into the intimidating mass of galaxy. The man started sharing with me for a time about the revelation that was about to be released to the church about the saints' access to heaven. I was thrilled to know that it was common knowledge throughout heaven that God was releasing this understanding to His bride on earth. When he saw how excited I was, we both started laughing and worshipped Jesus together for what seemed like hours.

After I talked with the man for a while longer, Holy Spirit spoke to me, He said; "Are you willing to step off the diamond platform with me?" I walked to the edge of the crystal floor and said; "I will go wherever you go Lord". I stepped off and didn't fall. I walked through the galaxy as though there was ground beneath me. I walked and observed the stars closer then I had ever dreamed I would. Holy Spirit then spoke to me and said; "Turn around!" I turned and saw Shawn standing on the edge of the crystal glass looking very sceptical. I started to wave at him and shouted; "Hey Shawn! How do you like heaven?!" He flinched when he heard my voice, but didn't respond or look up at me. He just stood with a conflicted look on his face for a moment, then turned around and walked away.

After the soaking time had finished, all of us met in a circle to share about what we felt God had shown us. The second it was Shawn's turn to share, his face quickly betrayed how awkward he felt. A few timeless seconds had passed before he started to talk. He shared that when he was spending time with God he had started to see a bizarre movie like vision in his mind's eye and that he wasn't sure if it was from God or not. He mentioned how in his mind he saw himself walking along something that looked like a large crystal floor in the shape of a diamond that was surrounded by the stars. He almost seemed embarrassed when he said that he saw a man standing on the platform who looked like he was glowing blue. He went on to say that at one point he was standing on the edge of the diamond when he heard someone shout, saying; "Hey Shawn! How do you like heaven?! He said that he didn't respond because he thought that he was just making the entire thing up in his head. I was laughing pretty hard by the end of his testimony and got to share with him that not only was I in the same place in heaven as him but that I was the one who had called out his name and asked him the question!

The Realm Of The Imagination

The imagination has gotten a lot of flack ever since the prophetic has been restored to the church. Sceptics would often say to people who have had visions things like, "Are you sure you didn't just imagine that?" When in reality, the imagination was most likely used in the process of someone receiving a vision or even a third-heaven encounter. This isn't a bad thing in the slightest. Our imaginations were given to us as a tool to help us encounter God. In my last testimony, my friend Shawn was a prime example of how God can use the imagination to lead us into encounters. Daniel said that he was troubled by the visions in his head, showing us that the realm of visions is in the mind. We need to trust that Holy Spirit is capable of leading us in all ways. This way instead of writing our imaginations off as something that's bad we can come to an understanding that it's a part of our design to help us in knowing our Daddy God better. While doing training and equipping ministry for the prophetic, it's always interesting for me to see that usually the most creative people like artists will be the first to get activated. They will be getting pictures from God right, left, and centre because they know how to receive from Him in the realm of the imagination.

He Who Has Eyes Let Him See

Before we go into in the next section, we are going to take some time to activate this teaching. This is important so I encourage you not to skip over the activation. We need to position ourselves as good soil to receive the Word of God. After we have received it the best way to properly steward the Word is to water it by activating it. If we don't do this then often the seed dies and we lose it. So, what I want you to do is to grab your Bible and go to a quiet place with God where it can be just you and Him. What we are going to do is we are going to learn how to tap into experiencing heaven. Get out of the mindset that you need to strive to have this type of experience. All of heaven is your inheritance meaning that it is a gift given to you because you are God's beloved son or daughter. You don't have to fight or contend for a gift because it has been freely given to you.

In the Bible it talks about how the angels ascend and descend from earth to heaven and back, but this isn't the case for you. You don't have to ascend and descend because you are ALWAYS seated in heavenly places in Christ. The work is done. All that you need to learn to do is open your spiritual eyes to see what has always been around you ever since you were birthed into salvation.

Alright, are you by yourself with God? If you are then pray this prayer out loud with me. "Lord, cleanse and activate my imagination. Activate my spiritual senses to experience heaven!"

Take some time right now to read a few of the chapters written below to get your imagination flowing a little bit. While you're reading them keep in mind that everything that is written in these chapters is what is actually going on in heaven around you right now. They aren't just stories; these are the reality of your present surroundings.

- Ezekiel 1

- Revelation 4

- Isaiah 6

- Daniel 7:9-10

- Genesis 28:12-22

Now relax and clear your mind. Begin to ask Holy Spirit to help guide you to experience heaven the way that He wants you to. Ask Him to lead you to see, hear, touch, smell and taste heaven. Trust Holy Spirit where He leads you.

- Wait in His presence

- What do you see? 2 Kings 6:14-17

Since God may use your imagination to show you things in heaven, you might begin to see images in your mind's eye. It may help you to meditate on what was seen in heaven in the verses that you just read over.

- What do you hear? Revelation 14:2

- What do you feel? Revelation 1:17

Even if you aren't seeing anything in your mind's eye Holy Spirit might be teaching you to use spiritual touch. Do you feel God touching you at all? Do you feel heat on your body? Any tingling? Any wind? Do you feel joy? Peace? Do you feel at rest? Remember, these are all manifestations and attributes of heaven.

- What do you smell? Song of Solomon 1:3

- What do you taste? Psalm 34:8, Ezekiel 3:3

- Now, write down what you experienced or saw

Heaven is at hand for you. You can see, hear, touch, smell and taste it whenever you please.

The Soul Man

In my experience learning to grow to a place of maturity in Christ, the hardest part of my three-fold being to develop has been my soul. Our soul is our centre of emotions which at times can be a difficult thing to tame to God's will. Although it may seem difficult, it is extremely necessary and can be done with ease when we stop striving and begin to rest in our Father's love.

We have talked about how it is important for us to have a developed spirit. However, we need to understand that every expression of man's spirit has to come through the filter of man's soul. The spirit, soul and body cannot walk or function independently from one another, but need to co-labour together as one so that we can walk in the fullness of whom God has created us to be. Until we have allowed Jesus to bring restoration to our soul it will be in direct conflict with our spirit. Even things like discerning or speaking prophetic words can become tainted by a wounded soul.

Hebrews 4:12 says; "For the word of God is living and powerful, and sharper than any two-edged sword, piercing even to the division of soul and spirit, and of joints of marrow, and is a discerner of the thoughts and intents of the heart."

The Word of God separates spirit and soul because the spirit longs for communion with God, where an undeveloped soul functions out of carnality and selfish striving. This is why King David would actually command his soul saying "praise the Lord, Oh my soul!" I praise God that He is the healer of the body. I love physical healings, but I have learned that miracles of emotional wounds of the soul are just as, if not more profound and impactful than broken bones mending. When the soul is restored it can partner with the spirit's constant pursuit to know the deep things of the Father's heart.

The Wound

A heart wound is an area in our soul where we haven't allowed the kingdom of heaven to have full rule and reign. These types of wounds usually begin to take place when either through a circumstance in life or through words that have been spoken over us have made us believe a lie about who we are. Often these wounds will begin to take shape in childhood. A person's childhood is an ordained time to learn and discover his or her identity as a son or daughter. It's a time for a person to be paraded by their parents and by their Father God because they are so loved and accepted just the way they are. The enemy wants to plant lies at an early age before truth sets in because he knows that when a revelation of true sonship rests upon even one person, they will greatly advance God's kingdom.

When we receive the seed of a lie it can stunt our soul's growth, stopping us from reaching maturity in our identity and at times our personality. If a young boy or girl is deeply hurt and because of the pain embraces a lie, that area of their soul may never grow up. They can't grow up because they can't see past the lie to see who they were truly called to be. Therefore they will live their lives at a standard that is far below the potential where God created them to live. Lies that we receive as labels and titles aren't something that we often just grow out of with age. The world teaches us to tolerate the pain of not knowing who we are and teaches us to dismiss insecurity as part of our identity. Since an area of the soul can't grow up until healing is brought, there are many children in the bodies of grown men and women whose souls haven't yet matured. As long as we allow ourselves to believe a lie we will feel the pain that the wound created and perceive the world through the lens of a still-hurting child.

Satan takes delight in seeing others suffer the way that he himself does. He is the master of confusion not only because he confuses, but because he himself is confused about who he is. He is the father of lies not only because he lies, but because he himself has embraced all lies. He wants sons and daughters of God to wear his lies as a mask so that they are unable to see the light that shines underneath; he himself masquerades as an angel of light trying to hide the fact that he no longer knows his true form or purpose. Our insecurities and wounds need to be addressed and dealt with. An important thing to note is that a heart wound is simply this - a lie that we have embraced. It is not something that is a part of us, it is separate because of what Jesus did on the cross and at any time we can make the decision to believe the truth of who God has created us to be. Our insecurities, fears and sin do not define us, God's love does.

I shared with you a testimony earlier about how when I was younger I would do evangelism and pray for long periods of time because I thought that I needed to fight and strive for God the Father's approval. When I told this story previously I summed it up in a nutshell, but this was something that I actually struggled with for years. This was a lie that I personally embraced, and a wound that I had to eventually confront. I believed that I was unworthy of my Daddy God's love. I didn't think that He was proud of me for who I was, but only for what I did. I felt as though I was abandoned and alone. My wound didn't only affect me but it also affected everyone I tried to walk in relationship with. Since I wouldn't receive Jesus in that specific wound I built a wall of over-spiritualism around my heart, not allowing anyone to see that I was actually in pain. Insecurity and shame dictated my life. I was so ashamed of who I was that I began to dismiss the fact that I even had a personality for a time. Through a fear of rejection I kept my distance from people until it came to the point where I didn't know how to relate with anyone at all. I was a classic Adam from Genesis 3:10, I was afraid because I was naked, so I hid.

Looking back now the incredible thing to me is that I could never see that I even had a problem. I was completely blind to what was going on internally. I would get around people who were solid in their faith and would instantly become intimidated. I would assume that they were doing something wrong and that they were the reason why I felt insecure. I would feel as though there was tension between me and that person even though the tension was really just within my own soul. It's incredible the excuses we will use to avoid examining our own hearts. Proverbs 21:2 says; "Every way of a man is right in his own eyes." We assume too quickly that everyone else has the issues and cast judgement when really a lot of the time we are just afraid to look inside the fortress we have built around our hearts. Sometimes we jump from relationship to relationship and the same issues keep coming up. We point and blame when really if we are seeing the same issues reoccurring, there is a good chance that the others aren't the ones with the problem. Or like I did, some of us jump from ministry to ministry or church to church, unable to commit because we are afraid to slow down, knowing that Jesus will be standing in the stillness, waiting for us to admit that we need healing and correction.

I understand church that this is a hard teaching to receive, but this is a part of learning how to sustain a revival. We have prayed fervently for years "send the fire of revival Lord!" and we have been right in praying this. We can be confident in knowing that with the fire of revival; miracles, signs and wonders will happen, the lost will be saved and set free, but we need to be mature in knowing that the fire of God also refines and chastens. Without leaders submitting to proper refining, revival will never be able to be properly stewarded.

Job 23:10; "(When) He has tested me, I shall come forth as gold."

It's Time To Stop Running

Everyone who is born of the kingdom of God is called as a leader, and as leaders we need to constantly have an internal eye to examine our hearts and motives. Remember Matthew 17 at the Mount of Transfiguration - Jesus took Peter, James and John up the mountain where they came into an incredible encounter where heaven overlapped the earth. They could see Elijah and Moses standing there with them as Jesus was transfigured before their eyes into a heavenly form. Peter responds to this encounter in an intriguing way, he says; "Lord, it is good for us to be here; if You wish, let us make here three tabernacles: one for You, one for Moses, and one for Elijah."

The reason why Peter wanted to build tabernacles was because in the Old Testament when the glory of God would come, it would always have to be contained within a tabernacle or tent to be sustained. See, Peter instantly went into ministry mode to try to contain the glory so that they could try to sustain the revival atmosphere they were experiencing. After this the Father spoke through a bright cloud and said, "This is My beloved Son, in whom I am well pleased. Hear Him!" The purpose of Jesus bringing the three onto the mountain wasn't for them to minister by building tents to contain the glory; it was for them to hear from the Father to receive an internal revelation about who Christ was.

If we allow our zeal to go before our wisdom like Peter in his younger years, we will try to push our way into ministry before God has intended it. We may see it as a destination and think that it will make us feel important and accepted when really we just need to stop running and deal with the inner work that God is trying to do. God the Father didn't speak this to the three for no reason. There was an internal revelation that needed to take root and a mindset that needed to be corrected before they could walk in their apostolic call to steward revival. Developing the inner man is part of the training. It isn't God's desire to have broken and defeated people going out to try to bring healing to a broken and defeated world. God wants sons and daughters to be solidified and complete in Him. The apostle Peter in his latter years said that we are all called as living stones to build a spiritual house (1 Peter 2:5). We won't be usable as living stones until Jesus the rock is first formed within us. He wants to take us from being reeds flapping in the wind to solid and un-cracked pillars for His kingdom. It's time to take our eyes off of the external for a moment and make sure that the proper internal formation of Jesus is taking place. It's time for us to stop running. If we want to be used as solid leaders, we need to deal with the issues at hand.

Moses was probably one of the greatest leaders in all of history; but when God commissioned him into his calling as a leader over Israel he was insecure in walking out his mandate. He feared that God couldn't use him because he couldn't speak with eloquence. God gave Moses the option to confront his wound, He said "go, and I will be with your mouth and teach you what you shall say" (Exodus 4:12). Instead of dealing with his heart issue by trusting God, he had asked God to send someone else. God counteracted by permitting Aaron to be Moses' mouthpiece. Since Moses didn't face his insecurity with his speech impediment while he was in the secret place with God, he had to fight his inner battle everyday as he walked as the leader of a nation.

After Moses had walked as the leader of Israel for a few years, God asked Moses to do something that triggered his insecurity. The Israelites had run out of water and began to ask God to provide for them. God spoke to Moses and told him to speak to a rock, saying that when he spoke, that water would flow from it. Moses had to either trust God that He would give him the ability to speak or he would have to compromise God's will because he was afraid. Instead of speaking to the rock, Moses hit it with his staff because insecurity dictated his decision. This wasn't a small matter in God's eyes. Moses had disobeyed the Lord and wasn't permitted to enter the Promised Land because of it.

We can see how Moses' wound stood in direct conflict with his promise and destiny. It's interesting to see how God offered Moses the choice to deal with this issue before he was given the platform in ministry. As a minister of the Gospel it can be hard to trust a leader who hasn't confronted his wound. Where there is a heart wound there is unbalanced emotion, and emotion that isn't mastered will cloud discernment. When we are in training for our callings, that is the time for Christ the foundation to be established in the inner man. Every crack must be filled and sanded so that we can be unshakable. After the foundation is laid and the training is complete God will begin to place the pillars of ministry on top of the foundation. A seamless and un-cracked foundation will steward the pillars properly. However, if there is a foundation that is still incomplete, all that it takes is one small shot at a sensitive crack and all the pillars can come falling down. This is why it's important to deal with the issues at hand before we try to deal with the bigger issues that are beyond us. The more platform and influence that we have, the greater the effect will be if we fall.

Jesus, Healer Of The Broken Hearted

God wants to surface our wounds so that He can bring restoration and healing to our soul. He will often surface a wound through situations that will activate the pain and discomfort of our insecurities and fears. Let me clarify something, I'm not saying that God will permit or cause pain. I'm saying that God will use a circumstance to unveil the fact that we are already hurting - there's a difference. Once we spot the wound we can simply receive the Father's love in that area of our hearts.

A lot of the time when we hear the words 'inner healing' we get freaked out because the term has been abused. Inner healing doesn't have to be a painful process, nor does it have to be long and drawn out. God is bigger than that. We don't have to climb the mighty mountain of inner healing, we can just fly above it on the wings of the Lord. The expectation needs to be that every time we bring a hurt to Daddy God that He will heal it. Not that He will heal it eventually, or that we have to contend for it, but that He will bring healing, peace and joy instantly. It isn't God's will for us to be in emotional distress and it isn't His will for us to be pinned down because of insecurity and fear of rejection.

Here's a scenario that provides a good example of how we can spot a wound and how we can begin to receive the love of the Father in our soul:

94

Say that you are praying with a group of friends and you begin to feel afraid to pray out loud. You start to feel an insecurity rising that says that your prayers don't sound as good as what others are praying. When this happens, there are two things that you can do. You can either sit feeling insecure and frustrated, or you can begin to stand on the Word of God which says that your insecurities and fears were taken away on the cross.

If you choose the latter, your first step is to ask God why you are feeling insecure or fearful. Ask God what lies you are believing about yourself to make you feel this way. When Jesus as a child asked the Pharisees questions in the temple, He was modelling for us that it's wise to ask questions (Luke 2:46-47). Every problem that we face, either internally or externally, can be a teaching to help us become more like Jesus if we choose to learn from it. Ask Holy Spirit questions. He isn't intimidated by them. When we ask God questions we are positioning ourselves as students, and when we position ourselves to be His students we give Him authority to be our Teacher.

Once you have spotted what the lie is, you have found the root of why you are feeling the way that you are. The lie is no longer a hidden secret in the dark corners of your heart, it is instead naked and exposed for what it truly is. When the lie is exposed, it is important that we forgive anyone who might have contributed to us believing the lie. When we don't forgive, we are taking ownership for someone else's actions. Unforgiveness always leads to bitterness, which hurts us more than the person who has wronged us. In order for us to experience the fullness of freedom, we need to learn to let things go.

After the process of forgiveness, this is when you can begin to ask God to help you see from His perspective. How does He see you in this situation? What is your Father saying to you? What words of comfort and blessing is your Dad speaking over you? Your Father is never going to speak anything negative about you. You are His beloved son or daughter. Ask Him to help you see yourself the way that He sees you.

Your next step is to begin to speak over yourself the truth of what your Father is saying about you. Proverbs 18:21 says; "Death and life are in the power of the tongue, And those who love it will eat its fruit." If you come into agreement with your insecurity, you are empowering it, so in order for us to eliminate the lie we need to speak life into ourselves. This is the same heaven-on-earth principal that we discussed earlier. There is no fear or insecurity in heaven, only perfect emotional freedom. It is never God's will for us to remain broken and afraid. When you declare truth over yourself and begin to believe it, you dethrone the lie because truth is established in your heart. The lie is no longer just exposed, it is eliminated. In doing this you are taking your thoughts captive and are commanding them to be transformed to God's will.

Every time I begin to feel insecure in any way I've made a point of learning to declare, out loud, the truth of what God says about me. If I start feeling insecure as a church leader, I'll begin to search out God's truth in the matter. I know that if He has called me then He has equipped me in His strength. So I'll look in the mirror and say, "Luc, you're a good leader because God is in you and with you always", and I'll keep saying that until I actually believe what I'm saying. God wants to re-pattern our way of thinking until we view ourselves the exact way that He views us. If you feel that your prayers are inadequate, speak over yourself that your prayers have power because you're a child of God. If you struggle with seeing yourself as attractive, prophesy over yourself the truth of how your Father sees you. Speak into yourself that you are beautiful, that you are accepted for who you are, that you are highly blessed and loved. If you have believed a lie that says you aren't smart, then start speaking over yourself that you are brilliant because that's the way that God sees you.

Jesus was the perfect example of someone who rejected all of the lies that the world assumed of Him and embraced all of the truth that the Father said about Him. When Jesus was baptized in Luke 3:21-22 God the Father spoke from heaven to Jesus the Son and said, "You are My beloved Son; in You I am well pleased." Since Jesus chose to believe the words that His Father spoke over Him, He was fully confident in who He was. He was completely solid and unshakable emotionally and mentally because what His Father said was established in the foundations of His heart.

Shortly after His baptism, Jesus was led by Holy Spirit into the wilderness where He was tempted by Satan for 40 days. It's interesting to see how the devil began to tempt Him in Luke 4:3. Right away he started by trying to sway Jesus from the revelation of sonship that He received from the Father by saying "If you are the Son of God..." But, Jesus allowed the truth of His identity to sink so deep within Himself that He was too confident to second-guess who He was. We are blessed that we serve a God who isn't in an identity crisis. He is the great I AM, because He is fully Himself and not willing to compromise His identity.

When we receive our Father's blessing, we can then begin to live our lives like sons and daughters. We can stand with confidence alongside of our brother Jesus that confounds the world's way of thinking. When we don't submit to the lies that the world says about us, we will face rejection and persecution. But, every bit of rejection will push us deeper into our Father's arms and we will see that the world's rejection is powerless in comparison to our Father's acceptance of who we are. Our Father accepts us just the way we are. When this truth sinks in; all jealousy, striving and competition are completely dethroned. This is when we know that Jesus the Son has truly been formed within us.

You are highly blessed and favoured. Your Daddy God is proud of you. You are His delight. He loves you just the way you are. He believes in your dreams. You are so beautiful to Him. You are brilliant. You are so precious, so priceless, so loved.

Mastering Our Emotions To Heaven's Will

I will finish this section of the book on this note: as we hear from Holy Spirit and learn to confront our wounds we begin to understand how to persevere through trials and suffering. As we learn to persevere character begins to take shape. This is the place where hurt and sway-able children cross into a place of being unshakable. Just as Ezekiel was given a head of flint (Ezekiel 3:9) to prevent the ideologies of the Israelites from penetrating his mind, Christ the rock is formed within our minds stopping the lies of the world from taking root. Someone who knows how to minister in the anointing and functions in the gifts of the Spirit can be very beneficial in advancing God's kingdom. However, a leader will never be able to steward what has been given to him until Godly character is established. Spiritual gifts can be taught and activated instantly, but the fruit of the Spirit takes time to grow. As our wounds are healed and solid character takes shape it becomes easier to take the focus off of ourselves to see the Father's will. Emotion that was once selfish and unbalanced is conformed to the flow of heaven.

Jesus was a complete Son in His being. He allowed all truth and love from the Father to be rooted in His heart and soul. He walked in complete freedom from any heart wound so therefore His emotions weren't dictated by insecurities or fears. His soul wasn't tied down by lies so therefore He could allow all of His emotions to come into perfect alignment with the Father's emotions. Matthew 14:1-16 gives us a good picture of how much Jesus was in control of His emotions.

In Matthew 14 Jesus' cousin John the Baptist was beheaded and John's disciples came to tell Jesus about his death. After receiving the news about His cousin's death Jesus went to a deserted place to spend time with His Father. Matthew 14:13-16 says; "He (Jesus) departed there by boat to a deserted place by Himself. But when the multitudes heard it, they followed Him on foot from the cities. And when Jesus went out He saw a great multitude; and He was moved with compassion for them, and healed their sick. When it was evening, his disciples came to Him, saying, 'this is a deserted place, and the hour is already late. Send the multitudes away, that they may go into the villages and buy themselves food.' But Jesus said to them, 'They do not need to go away. You give them something to eat.'" This of course was when Jesus performed the miracle to feed 5,000 people.

It is amazing to see how Jesus had complete mastery over His emotions compared to his disciples in this passage. Let's recap: Jesus just loses His cousin and desires to have time by Himself with His Father. While Jesus is in a state of mourning, masses of people come to Him wanting ministry. He begins to feel the compassion of His Father towards them. Jesus acknowledges His own emotions but chooses to look beyond Himself to the multitudes where His Father was looking. Just because the Father's heart was for the masses Jesus wouldn't take His eyes off of them, even though there was chaos in His own family life. His disciples began to sway from a place of faith and ministry to a place of concern for the people because they feared that they all would starve. Even in this Jesus knew that His Father's heart was turned towards the masses and He wouldn't take His eyes off of them. His heart was completely unswayable from what His Father's heart broke for.

I say all of this because quite simply there are times in ministry when we need to minister although our emotions are telling us to do another thing. We need to allow our souls to catch up with our spirits. I'm sure that the disciples weren't just concerned that the masses had no food to eat, but also that they themselves didn't have enough. This emotional sway for the disciples almost stopped a move of God before the Father wanted it to end. Their fears caused them to compromise the Father's will. It is very easy to see here that Jesus had mastery over His emotions but emotion had mastery over the disciples. As we come to a place of completeness in our souls there is grace for our emotions to come in constant alignment with our Father's just like Jesus.

The Natural Man

The last part of man's three-fold being that we are going to look at is the natural man, which is the body. The body is the outer core of man, the container of the soul and spirit and the temple of the Lord. Where the spirit and soul are not bound by age, the body walks along a timeline. It binds spirit and soul in covenant to the earth until the body itself passes on.

Every child of God is an extreme threat to the kingdom of darkness. Ecclesiastes 3:11 says; "He has put eternity in their (man's) hearts." Every one of us actually holds the potential to alter history and affect eternity forever; this is why it is one of the enemy's tactics of warfare to shorten man's timeline on the earth by killing the natural body through sickness and disease. If there is no body in the natural to be a bridge for the kingdom, then heaven's reign can't be established on the earth. The more that we allow God's reign to have authority within the natural man, the less sickness and disease can have a hold on us.

Isaiah 53:5 says; "But He was wounded for our transgressions, He was bruised for our iniquities; The chastisement for our peace was upon Him, And by His stripes we are healed."

The word 'transgression' in this verse comes from a Hebrew word that means 'sicknesses', and the word 'iniquities' comes from a Hebrew word that means 'pains'. So this verse literally says; "But He was wounded for our sicknesses, He was bruised for our pains; The chastisement for our peace was upon Him, And by His stripes we are healed." It is good news that we are completely healed through what Jesus did on the cross. He is a God who neither delights in pain, nor does He permit it. Our God isn't a God who wants to bring healing some of the time, He wants to bring healing every time anyone brings any form of pain to Him. Some might wrestle with the idea that God might permit sickness or pain to inflict our bodies to teach us or discipline us to make us more Christ like. I've even heard pastors at times thanking God for cancer because of the lessons they had learned by having it. Although this type of mindset seems somewhat logical, it is unbiblical.

The word Testament, as in 'Old Testament' and 'New Testament' comes from the Hebrew word 'Covenant' which is more accurately translated

'Contract'. So, in the Old Contract, all types of sickness, disease and pain had a place of authority over man because his sin stood as a solid wall separating him from *Jehovah-Rapha,* God the Healer. The story of Job is a popular account that people use to try and argue that God might permit sickness. However, since Job lived in Old Testament times, despite the fact that he was considered the most righteous man in the world in that time, he was still separate from God. Perfection was unattainable to him, which gave his sin power to bar him from God, meaning that sickness still had a place of authority over him. Man's closeness to God in these times was dependant on his ability to strive through works. Of course, man was incapable of perfection, so out of love, God became a Man and completed the contract that He had with Himself by fulfilling the law flawlessly. When He did this, every person who professed Jesus to be Lord was brought into a direct love relationship with God the Healer. All of our transgressions and iniquities were placed underneath the feet of Jesus.

Every believer now stands as a co-heir with Christ having complete authority over every sickness, disease and pain. To say that God would occasionally permit sickness or pain would be to say that they have a God-given authority over us, which would not only contradict God's Word, but would undo the works of the cross. Since pain was something that Jesus overcame and died for, it is defeated in its entirety. In New Testament times, if God permitted the occasional pain to teach us something, that would be the same as God not forgiving the occasional sin to teach us - when actually they were both atoned for on the cross. We need to understand that Jesus is our great Teacher, not sickness. Perfect health is our inheritance. Moses was a forerunner in this promise. Even in his latter years at the age of 120 his eyes were not dim at all nor was his natural vigour diminished.

As you are reading this, if you have any sickness or pain at all in your body, I encourage you to position yourself right now to receive. God wants to release waves of healing over you to bring healing into your body.

I declare an awareness over you right now of the presence of God. I command the body of anyone who reads this to come into direct alignment with the Word of God. All pain and sickness flees now. I release the kingdom of heaven to come and take reign in your body. Complete healing is your inheritance.

If you can, try and do something right now that you weren't able to do before. Test to see if the pain is still there.

Victory Over Death

We talked earlier about how when Adam lived in the Garden of Eden he was living in a place where heaven and earth dwelled together. Not only was Adam as a natural man immune from every sickness and disease in the garden, but I can't even bring myself to believe that death was something that God had intended for man to experience before the fall. I believe that since Adam constantly ate from the tree of life, he was so filled with the life of God that death couldn't even touch him. If we constantly eat from the tree of life (which is Jesus) it is impossible for death to have any foothold in our bodies at all. Death has lost its sting! Even after the fall, take a look at man's supernatural lifespan. The oldest man who ever lived was Methuselah, and he lived to be 969 years old. It wasn't until Moses' time that God had put an age restriction on us which was 120 years because of our sin and violence. As farfetched as this may seem, we profess that we can walk in the restoration of all things because of what Jesus did on the cross; so why not believe that it's attainable to live a life where death and age can't restrict us. Sin is no longer a reason to permit age caps because sin is defeated. A friend of mine once said; "The bride will ascend for the rapture not when she believes that she is defeated, but instead, when she knows that she is pure and spotless. The life of Christ will fill her to such an extreme that death won't be able to take her, so she will just ascend like Enoch did, never tasting death."

There were numerous men in scripture and in history who had come to this place of being so filled with the life of God where death could no longer touch their natural bodies. The prophet Enoch walked so close with God that his entire being just slipped right into heaven, never having to experience death (Genesis 5:24). A similar thing happened to Elijah when he was taken from earth to heaven in a whirlwind (2 Kings 2:11). There was a Middle-Eastern prophet who lived from the later 1800's until the early 1900's named Sadhu Sundar Sing. At the end of his life he went to walk with God throughout the mountains of India and was never seen again. Testimony tells us that he was taken to heaven just as Enoch and Elijah were. The same is thought of Moses since his body or grave were never found. Many traditions say that God permitted Moses to remain on earth to continue his ministry until he lived to the age of 120 (which was the age cap in the Old Testament) and then the Lord took him just as Enoch was taken. Some believe that John the Revelator still lives and has been commissioned as an intercessor on earth until Jesus comes back because of what Jesus said in John 21:21-23:

"Then Peter, turning around, saw the disciple whom Jesus loved (John) following, who also had leaned on His breast at the supper, and said, 'Lord, who is the one who betrays you' Peter seeing him, said to Jesus, 'But Lord, what about this man' Jesus said to him, 'If I will that he remain till I come, what is that to you. You follow me.' Then this saying went among the brethren that this disciple would not die. Yet Jesus did not say to him that he would not die, but, If I will that he remain till I come, what is that to you?"

It's interesting what Paul the apostle says in Philippians 1:23-24; "For I am hard-pressed between the two, having a desire to depart and be with Christ, which is far better. Nevertheless to remain in the flesh is more needful for you." Paul the apostle came to receive Jesus so firmly in his life to the point where death couldn't take him unless he willingly submitted to it. While Jesus was on the cross in Matthew 27:51; it says "Jesus cried out again with a loud voice, and yielded up His spirit." This verse doesn't say that death took Jesus, it says that Jesus yielded up his spirit. In order for death to take Jesus, He had to willingly submit to it since He had authority over it. He of course did this in radical obedience to the Father. After Jesus' resurrection, He ascended in the natural realm just as Enoch and Elijah. The same was said of the apostle Peter. History and tradition testify that many tried to kill him, but it wasn't until he left a town after being stoned when Holy Spirit spoke to him and told him that he was to be crucified in the town in which he had just left. In obedience, Peter went back into the town and was seized to be crucified. Peter then said to his captors that he was not worthy to die the way his Lord had died and demanded that he would instead be crucified upside down.

It excites me that God has made our natural bodies so capable of stepping beyond what the world sees as possible. Since Adam was sinless and was created in the image of God, I don't believe there were any restrictions or limitations on his being as a man. Not only was he impenetrable to sickness, pain and death, but most theologians believe that the Garden of Eden had to have been thousands of miles in vicinity, yet Adam tended and took care of all of it. To do this Adam probably had strength like Sampson, could run supernaturally fast like Elijah (1 Kings 18:44-46), and could even fly just as Jesus did when He ascended to heaven. He would have had access to his full mental capacity, permitting him to tap into the deep wells of intellectualism. Through faith even things like telekinesis must have been achievable for him (2 Kings 6:4-7). I have heard endless stories of Christians who have begun to tap into the potential of the human body. It is documented all throughout history that some Christian mystics in their times of prayer would at times begin to lift right off of the ground. They would hear from God just as Ezekiel did when he hovered in the air and would go into visions from God (Ezekiel 8:3).

I knew a man who when he was 10 years old, went to the Banff hot springs in Alberta. He was swimming in the pool, when without his mother knowing, her boyfriend came up to him and said, "Hey, did you know that it's possible for people to breathe under water? You should go into a corner where no one can see you and try sitting in the pool with your head under the water and start breathing in and out." He went in blind faith, oblivious to the fact that this was an attempt against his life. He sat under the water and began to breathe in and out. He would sit in the pool doing this for minutes at a time, unharmed, actually breathing under water.

This is obviously an incredible story of how a young child encountered God the Protector. However, I also believe that it speaks volumes about the capabilities of the body that God has given us when we have the faith of a child.

The Purpose Of The Natural Realm

Ecclesiastes 1:9 says; "That which has been is what will be, That which is done is what will be done, And there is nothing new under the sun."

When Solomon wrote this he was stating that everything we try to accomplish or discover has already been done, that man's striving apart from God has brought us into a society and culture of repetitiveness. However, I see another deep teaching hidden within this verse. As a people who are born of the natural realm we need to understand its purpose and function. The realm of the natural is the realm of manifestation. Since the body is the container of spirit, soul and the kingdom, the body becomes a bridge for the unique expression of all three to have voice within the earth.

Every word that we speak into the natural has already been spoken in the realm of the heart (Luke 6:45). Every time God uses us to declare His word, before it is heard in the natural, His word has already been spoken by Him in the realm of the spirit. Every time we move a body part to any degree we have thought about it first moving in the realm of the mind either consciously or subconsciously. Every move of God on earth has first been birthed by the Father's desire, so therefore was in existence in His heart and in heaven before it was seen on the earth.

Everything that is seen in the natural realm has already been done in another realm. This is why there is nothing new under the sun. Our bodies must be properly stewarded and taken care of otherwise the spirit, soul and the kingdom of heaven have no vessel to manifest through to impact the earth. The kingdom needs to move from the Holy of Holies, past the Holy place, the inner court and the outer court to bring freedom and justice into the earth. I will expand more on this revelation in the next section of the book.

Conclusion

Just as God the Trinity walks in relationship and co-labours together as one, so must we. Otherwise, we risk falling into the trap of becoming unevenly yoked within ourselves. If my natural man is mature, then my body will be in great shape, permitting me to live a long healthy life. But, unless I also have a developed soul, I will be unhappy because I will be incapable of walking in mature and proper relationships. If my soul man is mature then I might be emotionally stable, but if my spirit man isn't also prospering then I risk only becoming an intellectual who lacks his own spiritual experience. If only my spirit man is developed, then I will have revelation to engage and experience the heavens, but my zeal will outrun wisdom which tells me to look after my body's needs. Eventually my natural man will die before its time, unbinding my spirit and soul from the earth.

We need to be wary of becoming unbalanced in our three-fold being and allow Christ to be formed to fullness through experiencing Him in body, soul, and spirit. When we come to a place of maturity in our three-fold identity and allow the complete formation of Christ to take place internally, I am convinced that it is impossible not to steward well what God has given us. All of history is made up of two family trees; the family tree of the seed of Adam, whose fruit brings the knowledge of good and evil which is death; and the family tree of the Son of Man whose fruit brings truth and life. We are part of a royal lineage, seated in heavenly places far above sin and death. We are kings and queens of the garden that God has given us. Kingdom come on earth as it is in heaven. Reign within us, Amen.

Expanding Beyond The Garden

Freely As You Have Received, Freely Give

Luke 17:21; "The kingdom of God is within you."

As we grow in relationship with Jesus, the kingdom that is within us becomes firmly established in every area of our lives. Matthew 11:12 says that; "The kingdom of heaven is forcefully advancing, and forceful men will lay hold of it." Another translation says "the violent will lay claim of it." Since the kingdom is ALWAYS forcefully advancing, when we come in alignment with heaven, every part of our lives begins to excel forwards with it. Our gifts, talents, character, love, emotional stability, revelation, you name it, all move forward never stopping or losing pace. It isn't God's desire for our walks with Him to be like a roller-coaster going up and down. It's His heart for us to always be ascending closer to Him. When we come in sync with the kingdom not only do we see advancement in our own lives, but the kingdom eagerly desires to forcefully move beyond us to impact the world.

One of the best and most crucial ways for us to steward an internal revival is to freely give away what God has given us. The apostle Peter had such a revelation that the kingdom was within him where it couldn't help but pour out of him everywhere he went. Acts 5:15 says that Peter's shadow would just cast upon people and they would be healed of their sicknesses. Peter had such a solid understanding of who Jesus was in him, that the revelation couldn't help but overflow. I believe that there is about to be a drastic increase of understanding in the church to walk in greater power and authority then even the early church did. Awareness of the kingdom has been increasing exponentially across the globe. Still, with all that we have seen this is just the beginning of this great move of God. The Lion of Judah is roaring to the nations from within every believer. Instead of caging His passion we need to roar violently with Him. It's time for us to stop just pointing from revival to revival and begin to see that we ourselves are called to be a living and walking revival wherever we go.

After Adam and Eve were banned from the garden in Genesis 3:24, God placed cherubim at the east of the garden, and a flaming sword to guard the tree of life. When He did this, the kingdom was actually enclosed within the garden and God held the sword to guard the door determining if anyone could access it. After years went by, look at what Jesus says to Peter in Matthew 16:19; "I will give you the keys of the kingdom of heaven." The kingdom that was once hidden away was about to once again be experienced by mankind whenever they would please. See, the flaming sword (the key) that was once in the hand of God which locked the kingdom within the garden was now placed in the hands of His church. In Song of Songs 4:12, Lover (who prophetically symbolizes Christ) says to Beloved (who prophetically symbolizes the bride of Christ) "You are a garden locked up." Even though we now hold the keys, we remain a garden locked up, imprisoning the kingdom until we make the decision to turn the keys that Jesus gave us. The flaming sword is in your hand. Just as Jesus had complete access to the kingdom within, so do we. We get to complete the mandate with Jesus by taking the culture of the kingdom beyond the garden to be fruitful and multiply, to fill the earth and subdue it with the order of heaven.

The Onan Pitfall

Many times our instant opposition from moving forth in our mandate of expansion beyond self will be the Onan pitfall. Genesis 38 tells a story about how a man named Judah bore three sons who were named Er, Onan and Shelah. Er took for himself a wife whose name was Tamar. After Er had married, the Lord killed him because he was wicked in the sight of God. As was custom, Judah's second son Onan was instructed by his father to marry his brother's wife to raise up an heir for his brother. When Onan laid with his new wife, instead of emitting his seed within her, he would spoil it on the ground.

This is the first account in scripture that mentions any form of masturbation. The reason why masturbation is not a healthy practice is because when a man masturbates he isn't stewarding properly the seed that God gave him. Man's seed was given to him because it has the power to create life. In order for it to do so, it needs to be received by fertile ground so that conception can take place. When the seed is misused and is cast upon ground that isn't fertile in an act of independence, we are abusing our platform as co-creators with God.

The reason why I am saying this is because as the church we have at times given into the temptation of spiritual masturbation. I have seen many times when God has poured out over an individual or a congregation and they begin to walk into an incredible understanding of the kingdom, the glory and the power. Yet, the move of God would end prematurely because the presence wouldn't be stewarded properly by people who refused to share what was given to them. They would have a profound revelation of God's love for themselves so therefore would have many love encounters with Jesus, but wouldn't receive a revelation of salvation for those outside of the four walls of the church. This is spiritual masturbation because it is only using the seed that God has given us to please ourselves instead of releasing it onto fertile soil to see multiplication and any true fruit.

Remember the parable of the talents; if we don't use properly what has been given to us then it will be taken away. If we stop at our own victory then we are misusing the seed that has been given to us, preventing it from penetrating new land. We ourselves eventually become infertile and barren ground because the seed is never watered through activation. Faith without action is useless and eventually is lost when it isn't used. Just as Onan was later killed for his sin, we willingly make the decision for the seed of revelation to die within us. In many cases, this is when we give up our authority as co-creators. God has given us the revelatory seed of freedom which is to bring life by birthing not only a personal revival but also city-wide and global revival. If we have a revelation of who Jesus is then we can't be selfish by hoarding His love. We need to passionately show everyone that we come into contact with His everlasting love and affection.

I love personal glory manifestations, don't get me wrong. It's in God's presence that we are transformed, but it can't stop there. There always needs to be expansion and multiplication. Sometimes we can get so caught up with personal manifestation that we forget about our call to the lost.

Luke 10:17-20 says; "Then the seventy returned with joy, saying, 'Lord, even the demons are subject to us in Your name.' And He said to them, 'I saw Satan fall like lightning from heaven. Behold, I give you authority to trample on serpents and scorpions, and over all the power of the enemy, and nothing shall by any means hurt you. Nevertheless do not rejoice in this, that the spirits are subject to you, but rather rejoice because your names are written in heaven.'"

When the disciples came back after the great commission, they were overzealous about the authority that they had over the demonic. Jesus acknowledged what they said but then instantly told them that this wasn't something that they should rejoice in and pointed them back to salvation. See, there was something about the disciples' over-emphasis on spiritual manifestation that made Jesus uncomfortable. He had to correct them, knowing that if their focus remained on only the manifestations that their attention would have been taken off of the lost. This would have eventually stopped the sweep of revival that was taking place - whereas if they kept their eyes on the salvation of Christ, then they would eventually see the nations transformed through their ministry.

Releasing The Kingdom

Jesus was the perfect example of someone who would minister to others the freedom that He Himself experienced with the Father. He needed no man to testify of Him because every time people were with Him they were experiencing the kingdom. He was a living and walking encounter to everyone He came in contact with. If someone needed to be healed, Jesus would heal them. If someone needed deliverance from an addiction or from a demon, Jesus would deliver them. He walked in a full revelation of what He carried within Himself everywhere that He went.

Since the kingdom is in all of us, we all have authority to heal the sick and cast out demons just as Jesus did. We are called to be a sign and wonder to everyone we meet. When you walk into a room the atmosphere shifts and changes because of who you are in Christ and what you hold inside of you. When Jesus would go to heal the sick, He wouldn't go and pray to the Father that He would reach down and heal them. Jesus would instead come to a place of recognition of who He was and what He carried. When Jesus healed the sick He would acknowledge that perfect health was within the kingdom that was inside of Him. He would then release the kingdom over a person and the sickness would flee. Jesus didn't have to shout or be loud to pump Himself up when He did these acts of faith. He would just show up and the kingdom would come because He knew who He was.

Jesus did this throughout His entire ministry. Remember the story in Mark 4:35-41; Jesus and His disciples are on a boat fishing. Jesus fell into a deep sleep in the middle of the boat when a great storm started to stir. When Jesus was sleeping, He was experiencing the peace of heaven. His disciples began to panic for their lives and came to wake Jesus up. They said "Teacher, do You not care that we are perishing?" Now, watch how Jesus responds to this situation. He was just experiencing the peace of heaven in His sleep, so He spoke forth what He experienced and said "Peace, be still!" The peace that was in heaven was released through Jesus and was established on the earth, shifting His circumstance by stopping the storm.

Another time in Matthew 14, Jesus was with His disciples and the masses came to them. After a time of Jesus ministering it became late and the mass of people needed food to eat. All that they had were five loaves of bread and two fish. In verse 19 it says that Jesus looked to heaven and then broke the bread and the food began to multiply. Jesus first looked to heaven because He had to acknowledge that there was no hunger in heaven. Since He could see this heavenly principal by faith, He could then release this aspect of heaven by performing the miracle of feeding 5,000.

One time while I was leading an outreach in Calgary, Alberta, I took a group to one of the hospitals. We saw a woman sitting in a wheel chair wearing a cast. We approached her and asked her what had happened. She was very open about letting us know that she had an abusive boyfriend and the night before he was upset with her and threw her down the stairs. As a result she had broken her leg in two different places. I began to tell her that we were Christians, that Jesus loved her and that her leg would be healed if she let us lay hands on her. She seemed sceptical but let us do it anyways. In our hearts we acknowledged that there was no pain in heaven and began to release the kingdom over her. We placed our hands on her leg and I spoke forth, commanding the bones to come back together and declared that she was healed.

I told her to try and do something that she couldn't do before, so she put her foot on the ground and began to put pressure on her leg. She started freaking out because her bones had fused back together on the spot and the pain completely left. We stayed and talked with her for a while as she began to share with us that she was in prostitution and was trying to change her lifestyle. We spoke life into her and told her that we would be back in a few days to visit her.

When we came back to the hospital two days later, the woman whose leg was healed was sitting on a bench looking so excited as though she was going to jump right out of her skin. We asked her why she looked so happy and she started to tell us about how she had taken a test about a year ago for sexually transmitted diseases (STDs) and when the test results came back she had nine irreversible STDs. She said that one day after we had met her and declared healing over her that she took another test and the doctors said that all of her STDs had disappeared! She was completely healed and made whole. Not only that, but she told us that after we met her, three of her immediate family members who she hadn't been in contact with for over 15 years because of her situation in prostitution had contacted her.

It's amazing what will happen when God's kingdom is released into someone's life! When God's kingdom took reign within her, it gave Jesus authority to bring every area of her life into heaven's alignment. After she had such a radical experience with Jesus she instantly became the hospital's new missionary. She brought her friend to us who had major health problems asking if Jesus could help her. Her friend had a huge beet-red rash on her entire leg, and she was in a wheelchair because she damaged her ankle which was now held together by a screw. She said that she'd had shoulder pains for 18-and-a-half years and that it hurt so badly that if you even touched her shoulder she would rather be giving childbirth. Her right hand was in the shape of a claw due to arthritis and she also had a lump the size of an egg sticking out of her back.

The team and I came around her and laid hands on her. Instantly she broke down sobbing feeling the love of the Father. We watched as Jesus began to touch her rash. The pigment of her skin began to change from dark red to the natural colour of the rest of her skin right in front of our eyes. I grabbed her hands and helped her up out of her wheelchair. As she got up the screw in her ankle melted and her ankle was fully restored. As she started walking with me, she started to cry all over again saying that for the first time in 18-and-a-half years her shoulder didn't hurt. She let go of my hands and ran over to my friend to give him a hug. When she did this her hand that was in the shape of a claw straightened out to normal. As she went to sit back

124

down, she asked us to touch her back where the lump was and we discovered that the lump had completely disintegrated right off of her back.

God is so good! He never lets us down when we step out in faith and trust Him. Holy Spirit told me a long time ago that if I ever wanted to see Him move in power then I would have to start putting myself in situations where, if God didn't show up my reputation would be finished. I know that at times it can be a scary thing to step out in faith expecting God to show up, but the closer we come to God in the secret place, the more we begin to understand that releasing God's kingdom isn't just something that we are called to do, it's who we are. We can step out in faith knowing that God will show up not because He has any obligation, but because He is our best friend and He loves sharing His love with His children. Remember, when we see and understand God in the secret place, we see and understand ourselves because we are created in His image. It is in our DNA as sons and daughters to be supernatural, radical and loving just like our Father.

Stepping Out Of Our Boxes

I'm sure that you have experienced this a time or two: sometimes when you come into a new friendship or relationship with someone you can begin to feel certain expectations being placed on you. You can feel the pressure of a box of expectancy trying to be forced around you as an individual, knowing that if you step beyond its barriers you will face rejection. When this happens you have a choice to make, you can either stand in your identity and risk the possibility of rejection or you can submit to the box of expectation that threatens to encage your personality. Someone who hasn't fully become confident in their identity will usually submit to these expectations, compromising who they are.

Jesus faced the same challenge every time He was presented with an opportunity to release the kingdom. The Pharisees expected a Messiah to come. They tried to interpret the scriptures and created a box of expectancy in their minds of what they thought the Messiah should look like. Jesus came to earth and was so confident in who He was that He wouldn't try to awkwardly squeeze into their box, in fact He completely abolished it. I've said it before, Jesus is the great I AM because He is 100% confident in who He is, not willing to compromise Himself. We get to stand with Jesus in His confidence, giving us the boldness to live a life unashamed of who we were created to be. It is God's desire to use you. Sometimes when we become intimidated around specific people we go into a state of adaptation in our personality and zeal out of a fear of rejection. I am so thankful that we love and serve a God who isn't intimidated by anyone. He is the same God yesterday, today and tomorrow no matter who's around! He is willing to be the same God in the church as He is in the secret place, and He is willing to be the same God on the streets as He is in the church. When we aren't seeing God show up in our work places and in our schools, it isn't because He's too scared to show up, or even that He just doesn't want to move. Most of the time it's actually because we are afraid to stand in our identity as administrators of the kingdom.

There has been a false teaching that we have embraced in the church concerning God's sovereignty. Since God is seated as the King of kings; He distributes calls, mantles, anointings, gifts and talents in His wisdom, which almost seem like acts of randomness to us. This is what makes God sovereign. His way of thinking is above our understanding because we don't see the whole picture, instead we see in part.

If God isn't showing up in power in the sphere of influence He's given us, we often jump to the conclusion too quickly that it just must not have been His timing. We use the word sovereignty as a way out when really our sphere of influence is land entrusted to us by the Father, in which we are called to establish God's kingdom. We do the same thing with our dreams and calls. We at times dream really big with God, but when it comes time to stand we see that there's responsibility, risk and trust that needs to take place before we can see our dreams become a reality. Often we can slip into a passive state and use the excuse that it isn't God's will for the moment.

God is changing the ways that we expect revival will come. In the past we would pray for a move of the

Spirit in a way as though expecting fire to fall from the sky. We would say that revival was just around the corner, but then sit back and wait for it to come. Here's where the shift is happening: where before we would sit back and wait for it to fall, now we are learning that revival has already occurred in our hearts. So instead of praying and waiting, we are now praying and releasing. Revival isn't a sovereign decision of God that might possibly happen; revival is ALWAYS God's desire and will to be poured out to the nations through His church. His heart is for every individual, community, city, state, province, island, tribe and nation to experience His everlasting love. It's our decision in whether we are hungry enough to see heaven on earth. My words may encourage you in that direction, but how far you go for the kingdom depends on your willingness to begin to discover who Christ is in you.

Dealing with Offense

Every time that God begins to move in a new way there is always the potential for offense to swell. It is important to test the spirits of different manifestations by asking Holy Spirit and by bouncing it off of the Word. But, we need to be weary of labelling manifestations as false just because we don't understand them. Offense threatens to function as an obstacle that will stand directly in the way of us seeing a united move of God globally. To take offense is a choice just as it was in Jesus' days. In Bible times, Jesus would say things like "unless you eat the flesh of the Son of Man and drink His blood, you have no life in you" (John 6:53) without giving any sort of explanation or interpretation. Unfortunately many of Jesus' disciples allowed offense to enter their hearts and rejected Jesus' teaching saying that no one could understand it. As an after-effect of allowing their intellect to lead them before their hunger for life, they missed out on the truth in the teaching.

We are living in a day where God is releasing new signs and wonders throughout the nations and if we get offended, then we might just miss Jesus. We brand miracles, signs, wonders and the prophetic as being unscriptural when I'm sure that the Pharisees said the same thing about what was seen while Jesus was on the earth. Since the New Testament wasn't written yet when Jesus came, people only had the Old Testament to refer to. I'm sure that the Pharisees labelled Jesus as a heretic when they didn't see walking on water or bread multiplying in the Old Testament. We need to be careful of making the same mistake of writing off the new signs and wonders that God is releasing in these days. If there is any offense in our hearts towards the things of God we need to repent and come on board with what He is doing. To repent simply means to change the way that we think. God spoke to me a long time ago and told me that if I wasn't on board with what He wanted to do in the nations or if I had allowed offense to enter my heart, He would move anyways and give my calling to someone else.

When we reject new teachings inspired by Holy Spirit we aren't just rejecting the words being spoken, we are rejecting Jesus the Teacher. In turn, if we reject miracles from God we are rejecting Jesus the Miracle Worker. I am convinced that when we criticize a manifestation from Holy Spirit we are closing doors for us to experience those same manifestations of love from Jesus in our own lives. But, if we come to a place in our hearts where we turn from our offense, then we receive the grace to experience God in the same way that we were once offended by Him.

Kingdom Invasion

We are going to do an activation right now where we learn how to release the kingdom of heaven. When we live in faith, we can see heaven take reign in every circumstance where it's attributes are scarce, just as I shared earlier about Jesus establishing peace and an end to starvation. I encourage you to practise kingdom declaration in every area of life; however, in this activation I am going to teach you specifically how to release the kingdom of heaven to see the sick healed. We get the great privilege of being representatives of heaven, meaning that we have the opportunity to be Jesus to people in every situation. Jesus was a vessel who ushered salvation in its fullness through kingdom invasion. Since He is our leader and commander, we are called to follow His very steps.

Mark 16:17-18 says that; "These signs will follow those who believe: In My name they will cast out demons; they will speak with new tongues; they will take up serpents; and if they drink anything deadly, it will by no means hurt them; they will lay hands on the sick, and they will recover."

This verse doesn't say that these signs will follow only those who are prophets or apostles, but instead to those who believe. We see here that it's not only some who are chosen to be used to release the kingdom to heal, but that every believer has the authority to lay hands on the sick and see them recover. This is the commission of every Christian now just as it was in Jesus' times. We are all called to expand and claim dominion beyond the garden.

Jesus said at the great commission in Matthew 10:7-8; "As you go, preach, saying, the kingdom of heaven is at hand. Heal the sick, cleanse the lepers, raise the dead, cast out demons. Freely you have received, freely give."

Notice how in this verse it doesn't say to heal some of the sick; it just says to heal the sick. When Jesus' disciples were commissioned to preach and demonstrate the kingdom they were released by Jesus to heal EVERY sick person that they came in contact with. God's heart is always for people to be set free and His desire is to do this through His church. Matthew 12:15 says; "Great multitudes followed Him, and He healed them all." Jesus didn't heal some, He healed all. Our expectation needs to be that when we pray for people to be healed that they will recover every time. Some might argue that only some are called to see the sick healed since 1 Corinthians 12 talks about how Holy Spirit distributes gifts of healings to some. I do agree that some have more of a call to a ministry of healing, however, the Bible clearly states that this is something that every believer is called to walk in.

Just so that you know, I didn't always see such extreme miracles like in my previous stories. It took me time to grow into the revelation that not only did God still do these things today, but that He actually wanted to use me to do them. When I first received the revelation that God still heals and delivers today, I started to step out in faith to see the miraculous. For the first while I didn't see any miracles at all because that's just where my faith was at that point in my life. I told God that I would pray for as many people as it took until I began to see people set free. I stood on the written Word of God which told me that the same Spirit that lived in Christ that raised Jesus from the dead, lives in me. So therefore, if I kept praying for people, I knew that it was impossible for me to not eventually see the sick healed. I prayed for probably over 100 people without seeing a healing until I started seeing results.

An amazing part of being a leader in the church is that I get the privilege to allow everyone who receives my teachings to use my ceiling as their floor. This means that since you're receiving this teaching into your heart, you get to start where I left off in learning to walk in the anointing. I don't believe that you will have to pray for 100 people before you start to see healings if you begin to water this revelation by activating it. That being said, I'm going to give you a quick run-through in how to release the kingdom to see results. If you actually do this activation, it will help you to grow in the revelation of the kingdom more quickly than if you read this teaching I've written 10 times over, so I encourage you to step out in faith and expectancy.

1. Find someone who is sick or someone who is in pain. Anything from a headache to cancer, God wants to heal it all. Every sickness and pain has to bow to Jesus. Even try this on yourself if you need healing for anything.

2. If it is the appropriate time, ask the person if you can lay hands on them. Power and the kingdom can come from the hands. Habakkuk 3 describes the image of God and says that lightning bolts shoot from His hands. Since we are made in His very image we can also release the power of God through our hands (Acts 8:18).

3. I am convinced that it really doesn't matter what you say when you're praying or declaring as long as you have faith and your heart is in the right place. However, it is good to note that there is great power in declaration (Proverbs 18:21). A lot of times I will just speak forth "be healed" or declare that I am releasing God's kingdom. I also at times will command pain and sickness to leave or will command the body part that is hurt to come into alignment. Sometimes I won't declare or pray anything, I'll just tell the person to start trying to do something that they couldn't do before in an act of faith. Whatever you do, keep it short. You don't have to try and move God through lengthy prayers because He was already moved at the cross. In fact I've noticed that if I were to pray long prayers while believing for a healing that it gives a lot of room for doubt to come in which could prevent the miracle from coming.

4. Get them to test it out. After you declare healing over them, get them to try to do something that would usually trigger the pain. There is something about getting people to activate their faith that moves heaven. Remember when Jesus was speaking in the synagogue and there was a man with a shrivelled hand. Jesus spoke forth and told him to stretch out his hand in faith. Since he had the faith to test it out, when he stretched out his hand it was completely restored (Luke 6:6-10).

When you do this, one of three things is going to happen: Either they are going to be completely healed, they are going to be partially healed or they will still feel the same. If they don't notice a change or if they only feel some of the pain leave, then pray another short prayer and get them to test it out again. Remember when Jesus touched the blind man's eyes in Mark 8:22-26? After the first time, the man saw men that looked like tree's walking around because he didn't receive his full healing. Jesus touched him a second time and his sight was completely restored. If it took two tries for Jesus to heal someone, then don't feel any shame praying for someone two, three, or even ten times until they are healed. I believe Jesus did this to set an example showing us that it's alright to keep believing for a miracle.

As we are activated to receive and release the kingdom it's important for us to not stop in just having one encounter. I've led a lot of outreach ministries and it still surprises me how there is at times such a lack of drive for power evangelism. If I do a training and equipping school on the prophetic or how to experience the glory people will come left, right and centre. But, as soon as I have a school geared towards equipping the saints to reach the lost, people suddenly seem pretty scarce. Unfortunately, often the ones that do come out stop coming after seeing one or two miracles. The only way to steward a move of God is to fall in love with the lost. As soon as God starts using us in the miraculous we need to step up to the responsibility of being faithful with what He has given us, because we will be held accountable to the revelation that we have received.

When Israel was being chased by the Egyptians, Israel came to the Red Sea and began to cry out to Moses to deliver them. In turn, Moses turned to God to seek out their escape from Pharaoh. God's response rocks me to the core: Exodus 14:15-16; "And the Lord said to Moses, 'Why do you cry to Me? Tell the children of Israel to go forward. But lift up your rod, and stretch out your hand over the sea and divide it. And the children of Israel shall go on dry ground through the midst of the sea.'"

In this verse, God was holding Moses accountable to the revelation that He had already received. Moses already had a revelation that God was capable of using him in signs and wonders. Moses also already had a revelation that God was the Deliverer. So, instead of God just delivering Israel, He confronted Moses by asking Him why he was even crying out to Him in the first place. He then told Moses to walk in the revelation that he already received by lifting up his rod and performing the wonder.

Living a Lifestyle of Wonder

It's important that as we begin to move in the power of Holy Spirit that we never lose our sense of wonder towards God. One time, after I was finished speaking at a meeting, I invited people from the congregation up to the front to receive prophetic words.

I went from person to person giving words like I usually would, not thinking much of it. When I was finished, a dear friend of mine walked up to me and gave me a simple word from the Lord that completely transformed my way of thinking.

He said to me; "Luc, you need to understand that every word from God you speak and every healing that God uses you in is something that is precious to the Father's heart."

I looked behind me and realized that had I just left a trail of people crying because they were so touched by what God had said to them through me, but I somehow remained completely unaffected emotionally. Even though I was the one laying hands on people, I was missing seeing Jesus in each encounter.

When we begin to step out in faith and see the kingdom come, we can either allow ourselves to become numb to God showing up or we can make the choice to see Jesus as He encounters the people we are ministering to. When we make the choice to see Him, we are deciding to encounter Him. This way every healing manifestation that we see and prophetic word that we speak begins to transform us to look more like Jesus. I've probably seen hundreds of backs healed, but I still get extremely excited each time God does it. I get excited because it isn't just a back getting healed; it's a life being transformed. Never let God moving become something that you casually overlook. Every time He uses you He is entrusting to you something that is precious and priceless to His heart.

The Emerging Elisha Generation

Having A Teachable Spirit

1 Corinthians 4:15; "For though you might have ten thousand instructors in Christ, yet you do not have many fathers; for in Christ Jesus I have begotten you through the gospel."

As we start living a life that is in pursuit of God's kingdom we are making the decision to walk upon a greater platform of holiness. To be holy simply means to be set apart. Culture that once shaped our morals, character and personalities is left behind as the culture of the kingdom takes its proper place of influence. What once made sense to us will now seem like foolishness. When we see someone who is sick, we no longer perceive their suffering as a permanent reality. It is now seen as an injustice, which can easily be brought into proper order because of what was accomplished at the cross. A lack of finances no longer will seem stressful because we know that all of the riches of heaven are our inheritance. The patterns of our minds begin to take new course. What was once our basic ground of logic begins to shake and crack, proving to be false, for a new foundation of truth has been laid which reasons that the impossible is probable through Christ.

Everything I have written previously in this book has been about how to steward a revival in the inner man. Even the section on releasing the kingdom was just as much a sermon on tending the garden as it was about kingdom expansion, since expansion is crucial for personal stewardship. Although we have covered a lot of ground, the teaching is still incomplete. In order for us to come into a place of maturity, we need to be clothed with humility to the point where we are willing to be studious around those who have gone before us. There is a revelation of discipleship taking root in the heart of the church that stretches beyond mentorship and advances into the realm of fathering and mothering. If we are to truly live from a kingdom perspective we need to stop viewing the church as an orphanage and start seeing it as a family. Malachi prophesied that when Elijah came, he would turn the hearts of the fathers to the children and the hearts of the children to their fathers. In these days as the spirit of Elijah is resting upon the church, this very thing is happening.

Malachi 4:5-6; "Behold, I will send you Elijah the prophet before the coming of the great and dreadful day of the Lord. And he will turn the hearts of the fathers to the children, and the hearts of the children to their fathers,"

2 Kings 9-13; "Elijah said to Elisha, 'Ask! What may I do for you, before I am taken away from you?' Elisha said, 'Please let a double portion of your spirit be upon me.' So he said, 'You have asked a hard thing. Nevertheless, if you see me when I am taken from you, it shall be so for you; but if not, it shall be not so.' Then it happened, as they continued on and talked that suddenly a chariot of fire appeared with horses of fire, and separated the two of them; And Elijah went up by a whirlwind into heaven. And Elisha saw it, and he cried out, 'My father, my father, the chariot of Israel and its horsemen!' So he saw him no more. And he took hold of his clothes and tore them into two pieces. He also took up the mantle of Elijah that had fallen from him, and went back and stood by the bank of the Jordan."

The Elisha generation is the generation that is teachable because they learn from those who have gone before them. If we become puffed up with pride we will miss out on the rich heritage that the forerunners and our forefathers have left for us. It's interesting that in this passage Elisha actually calls Elijah 'father' instead of teacher or mentor. The fact that the church is a family instead of an orphanage is a beautiful thing. When we can honour our spiritual leaders as fathers and mothers, instead of just receiving their teachings, we actually receive an inheritance from them. If Elijah were only Elisha's teacher, Elijah would have only left behind teachings and parables for his pupil. However, since Elijah was Elisha's father, after his ascension, Elijah left an inheritance for his son. There is a very notable difference.

I am always encouraged to read about how both Elijah and Elisha honoured one another within their father and son relationship. Before Elijah ascended, Elijah as the forerunner honoured Elisha by asking him what he had wanted from him before he ascended. This needs to be the heart posture of every father. A true father will always be able to dream beyond himself. He will enrich himself spiritually not only for his own effect, but as an act of considering the generations to come. Therefore, as his own life is enriched, so is the heritage that he leaves behind.

Elisha honoured Elijah by acknowledging that he had something that was worth asking for. Elisha did a really good job of modelling a heart posture that was teachable. Here's a good tip for anyone that is wanting to come to a constant state of growth; if you notice that someone has something that you want, whether that's anointing, wisdom, love, platform, or whatever else: stop talking about yourself to try and make yourself look good in front of them and start talking about them. Ask them questions. Don't submit to any form of insecurity or intimidation that says you need to start to talk yourself up to be received by them. Acknowledge what they have, and start pulling on their anointing. This way instead of striving for their approval you are positioning yourself as a student while around them. As a leader I will more quickly commit to fathering someone who asks me questions compared to someone who constantly talks to me about how anointed they are. Don't get me wrong, it's not that I favour one person above the other; but I believe in being a good steward of my time and how well someone honours shows me how teachable they are.

I always encourage those who I father to have as many fathers and mothers that they can find. No one is going to be perfect in every area, so we can't assume that anyone will be a perfect father or mother. I try to have someone who is more experienced than me to pour into my life in any area where I want to see growth. I have people fathering and mothering me in my relationships, my finances, how I minister - you name it. It's a fascinating thing that we all only see and know in part. This means that instead of assuming the role of an expert, we get the privilege of positioning ourselves as students, constantly getting to learn from one another. Fathering and mothering has nothing to do with age. If you notice that someone younger than you is walking in a revelation that you don't understand, I would encourage you to take a studious posture. I am proud to say that I have grown and have been challenged greatly from the youngest of those that I myself father. I love Jesus' teaching to His disciples in Matthew 18 concerning this:

Matthew 18:1-3; "At that time the disciples came to Jesus, saying, 'Who then is greatest in the kingdom of heaven?' Then Jesus called a little child to Him, set him in the midst of them, and said, 'Assuredly, I say to you, unless you are converted and become as little children, you will by no means enter the kingdom of heaven.'"

Isn't that brilliant? Jesus' disciples come up to Him, trying to compete and one-up one another, so what does He do? He pulls a child in front of them and says, "This little kid understands something about my kingdom that you don't yet." What a lesson on humility and honour. Only when we are humble enough to honour someone for what God has given to them, can we receive an impartation of what they have.

Remember what Elijah said to Elisha after Elisha asked for the double portion; "You have asked a hard thing. Nevertheless, if you see me when I am taken from you, it shall be so for you; but if not, it shall not be so" (2 Kings 2:10). Just as Elisha watched to see Elijah touch heaven, when we honour those who have gone before us by acknowledging how they touched heaven throughout their lives, then we will receive the double portion. This is one of the reasons why there is importance in studying church history. When we read of what God did in the past, we honour the vessels. Their spiritual achievements become our own as we learn to stand on the shoulders of giants. When we do this as one body throughout the course of history we make the decision to be a spiritual house continually ascending higher, whereas a generation who chooses to be fatherless attempts to try and rebuild foundations that other men and women have already laid years ago.

Tradition tells us that Elijah was taken up in a fiery chariot, but that isn't what this passage actually says. Look at this; 2 Kings 2:11; "Then it happened, as they continued on and talked that suddenly a chariot of fire appeared with horses of fire, and separated the two of them; And Elijah went up by a whirlwind into heaven." The fiery chariot actually separated Elijah from Elisha, and then he was taken up by a whirlwind. I find it intriguing that God would send something so flashy like a fiery chariot to separate them when Elisha needed to see Elijah ascend to receive the double portion. It's almost as though God was testing Elisha to see if he was able to keep his eyes on the prize even though there was a distraction right in front of him.

While studying the lives of past men and women of God, I've found great value in searching out all aspects of how they touched heaven. We need to acknowledge the miracles, signs and wonders as well as how they touched heaven in their relationships and character. There is a temptation to only acknowledge the achievements that were flashier throughout their ministries since it is bold and in your face. However, there are also secrets of wisdom and strong leadership that are waiting to be discovered throughout the stories of the lives of our forefathers.

One of the most well-known leaders from the 'Voice of Healing' movement was Smith Wigglesworth. I'm sure most of you have already heard or read stories about his extreme faith and about the thousands of people who were healed and saved throughout the course of his ministry, so I won't go into detail. If you haven't heard any stories, look him up. You will get rocked and challenged, guaranteed. Before I studied Smith's life I had heard many teachers and evangelists share numerous incredible stories about the miracles, signs and wonders that he walked in. However, after studying his life I was surprised that I hadn't also heard from them stories about the extreme compassion and Godly character he had. While his testimonies of mighty acts of faith still echo throughout revival circles, the stories that spoke of his unconditional love and grace seemed to have been forgotten. It was beautiful reading about a man who operated in such boldness because he was moved with compassion.

The same is true of the great reformers that led the church out of a doctrine of legalism into a revelation of grace. Many of their lives have been forgotten by the church when in my opinion, their tremendous integrity and character go unmatched by anyone that I have ever met or read about. All aspects need to be considered in order for us to be properly fathered into becoming mature leaders.

Receiving The Five-Fold Ministry

Ephesians 4:11-12; "And He Himself gave some to be apostles, some prophets, some evangelists, and some pastors and teachers, for the equipping of the saints for the work of ministry, for the edifying of the body of Christ."

In order to position ourselves to be properly fathered and mothered, we need to gain revelation into how to receive from the five-fold ministry. Every person God calls as part of the five-fold ministry wears the mantle of a forerunner, because everyone who walks in one of these five office callings, even for a short amount of time, has gone ahead with the Lord to receive insight to train and equip the saints. They are God's stationed government within the church and they need to be embraced as family in order for us to see heaven's full reign on earth, both individually and throughout the nations. When we can learn to be fathered and mothered by the fullness of God's stationed government in the church, we will be brought into a proper balance in our being.

In Acts 1 it tells us how the eleven remaining apostles came to the conclusion that someone needed to come alongside of them in replacement of Judas. The apostles chose two men who had been with them while Jesus walked the earth who they considered worthy of the call to apostleship. They cast lots to see who would fill the abandoned platform and the lot fell on Matthias. This is when God's apostolic government came to a place of wholeness. Now, we see right in the next chapter that a great outpouring of the Spirit takes place and revival begins to be seen through the early church. It's important to note that before God showed up and the kingdom began to take reign in the land through the early church, that church government needed to be brought into God's order. Since the five-fold ministry is God's selected governing leadership, in order for us to see a genuinely advancing move of God, it must be stationed in its proper position within the body.

There is a shift that is happening within the church as God restores the revelation of the five-fold ministry. There used to be a mindset where congregations felt as though if they positioned themselves in submission to their pastors and leaders, they could only serve those specific visions. All of the peoples' strengths and anointings would be poured out constantly to create a good service for Sunday morning and those who weren't pouring into the meeting would sit as observers. Yes, we need to submissively serve our leaders, but we also need to understand that we aren't abandoning our personal callings by doing so. All of us have been given a place of influence to establish God's kingdom whether that's at school, in government, our businesses, through media, or in our families. We can't allow the platform that has been entrusted to us to become neglected and stagnant. When a congregation feels that its only mandate is to be pouring into their leader's vision, that leader as a vessel becomes the singular outlet to impact the world. If the kingdom's outlet is only one individual's vision, it limits God from flowing through the rest of the body in the spheres of influence they are entrusted with.

I feel as though I need to stress this point so that what I am saying isn't misconstrued. As members of a corporate body we need to humbly submit to our leaders and serve them diligently, bottom line. However, clarity needs to sink in that when we do this, we aren't handing over our personal dreams and passions on a silver platter. In fact, the only way for us to be fully released to walk in the call that God has given us is when we come under proper covering. Under proper covering our gifts become amplified. Just as the congregation is to serve the vision of the leaders, as the five-fold ministry is restored in the church, the leaders are in turn also to serve the visions of each individual in the body. As a leader in the church I am very quick to pour into someone's vision when I can see that they are willing to serve and submit. In God's kingdom no one is more important than another based on their callings or giftings. We all stand on the same playing field, side by side playing the role of servants to one another.

Read again what Ephesians 4:11-12 says; the five-fold ministry is "for the equipping of the saints for the work of ministry." Who is it that is to do the work of ministry? It's the saints! The saints need to serve their leaders, but in part the five-fold's job is to train and equip the saints so that they can see kingdom invasion in their places of authority. In doing so they serve the individual visions of the church members which is crucial since they are the ones who are positioned strategically in the marketplace. The kingdom's outlet to the world widens drastically when every person in the church becomes an outlet. Not everyone is called to be either an apostle, prophet, evangelist, pastor or teacher. Each five-fold minister is a gift to the bride of Christ, commissioned to beautify her to be pure and spotless before the nations by equipping her through their own ministerial expression.

The five-fold ministry are the five living stones who have allowed Jesus the rock to be formed within them. When they can move as one leadership unit in the church, the Goliaths of the land will be slain and conquered, giving the new Israel its rightful stage before the nations.

We will take a brief look at each of these calls to gain some understanding of God's order in leadership. This isn't a detailed teaching on the five-fold ministry, but instead is a brief overview of each call so that we can know how to receive each of their ministries in our lives.

The Office Of A Teacher

A teacher's function in the body of Christ is primarily operating as the mind of the church. God has stationed teachers as part of the five-fold ministry to get people rooted in the written Word of God. There is a grace over teachers to receive and release the ministry of Spirit of Wisdom, Revelation and Knowledge. This means that they can pull pivotal truths out of the Word of God with ease and present it with authority. Acts and some of Paul's epistles mention a man named Apollos who was a radical teacher back in the early church. Paul said in 1 Corinthians 3:6 that as an apostle he would plant, and Apollos would water the church through his teachings because he was a man of a fervent spirit and eloquence (Acts 18:25-26). It is necessary to have multiple teachers in a congregation since we understand in part. It is better for many teachers to be receiving and teaching revelation because then God can cover more ground with truth instead of only having one teacher who is expected to have a full revelation of all things.

For teachers there is a natural ability to take heavenly principles and to explain them in a way that people will be able to understand. I believe that Jesus the Teacher spoke in parables for two reasons: one of the reasons was because He wanted to hide the truth of what He was saying from the proud. Jesus would teach revelation through metaphors knowing that only those who were humble enough to seek understanding in the parables would find the truth. The other reason why He spoke in parables was because He was trying to teach the people heavenly principles and He had to use a language that they would understand. He couldn't approach the masses by talking about heaven the way He experienced it, because they would have had no grid of comparison to understand what He was saying. This is why He would compare the kingdom of heaven to a thing like farming which was a common industry in that culture. He met them where they were at. Teachers have the ability to take profound truths from the scriptures and explain them in a way where whoever they are speaking to will comprehend.

Just like every part in the five-fold ministry a teacher's job is to equip the saints for the work of ministry. They equip the church by teaching the Word, but they are also called to equip by teaching the rest of the body how to tap into revelation as easily as they themselves do. This is a crucial part of this office, otherwise a congregation's spiritual food will only come second hand from the teacher. We all need to know how to encounter Jesus through the written Word. It doesn't matter if you are a leader in the church, a business man, or a high school student, if we are children of God we need to be deeply rooted in the Bible.

Teaching ministry really helps balance out the prophetic to create solid men and women who are completely rooted in the written Word and engulfed in the Now Prophetic spoken word of God. They can't function properly if they are independent of one another. They need to partner as the double edged sword. If you are reading this and you are called as a prophetic leader, it is of great importance that you surround yourself not only with prophets to sharpen your gift but also with teachers, because you will never walk in your full potential without them. In turn, it's important for people who have more of a tendency to receive mentorship from teachers to branch off into being fathered by the other four ministries.

Two of the pitfalls that teachers need to keep an eye out for is a mindset of legalism and intellectualism. These ditches can be avoided if we simply allow ourselves to balance out by surrounding ourselves with people who gravitate to different personalities and callings. There are some excellent teachers in our Bible colleges, but unless some of the other offices like the office of the evangelist walks alongside teachers, there is going to be potential for the Word to become knowledge without action. The call or anointing of a teacher can also at times rest upon a pastor, evangelist, prophet or apostle since all are called to train the body, and teaching is one of the most common techniques to impart information.

The Office Of A Pastor

There has been a lack of understanding in these past years concerning the five-fold ministry. In many ways the full burden to train and equip the saints has been placed upon the shoulders of the pastor. In the past, pastors have been expected to operate as the full embodiment of the five-fold. However, we are transitioning into a time where the church is ready to receive the rest of God's leadership, meaning that pastors will be relieved from this unpractical expectation. Where teachers walk as the representation of Jesus the Rabbi, pastors get the privilege to minister as representatives of Jesus the Shepherd. Teachers take more of a role in watering the church whereas pastors lean more towards protecting and nurturing the sheep. One of the best descriptions of a pastor that I've found in the New Testament is in Acts 6.

Acts 6:1-3; "Now in those days, when the number of the disciples was multiplying, then arose a complaint against the Hebrews by the Hellenists, because their widows were neglected in the daily distribution. Then the twelve summoned the multitude of the disciples and said, 'It is not desirable that we should leave the word of God and serve tables. Therefore, brethren, seek out from among you seven men of good reputation, full of the Holy Spirit and wisdom, whom we may appoint over this business;'"

I believe that these seven appointed by the apostles were the first to walk in the pastoral office in the early church. Most peoples' understanding of the pastor's primary anointing is to prepare and share the message with the church, when to be honest I don't even think it's necessary for a pastor to have to be the one to share on a Sunday morning, unless God has called and anointed him or her to do so. Where a teacher might spend the bulk of his ministry in studying and teaching, the pastor's burden is to be in amongst the people taking care of their practical and emotional needs. They will be the ones who are making sure that everyone in the congregation has enough money to buy groceries, making hospital visits to spend time with those who are sick and are willing to walk husbands and wives through relational issues. They stand as protectors and peace keepers amongst the church, just as a shepherd protects the sheep from the wolves and keeps peace amongst the sheep so that they can live together as one unit.

A part of the pastoral ministry is building Christ within the souls of individuals by bringing emotional balance and healing. This is why the pastors that were appointed in Acts 6 were called to take care of the widows. Pastors have a deep compassion and concern to connect the broken-hearted with the Father. The root revelation that pastors have to minister from is the revelation of the Father's love. Since this is the pastor's burden they will usually be involved in walking people through their heart issues through counselling, inner healing sessions and by living day by day with people in close relationship. Some of the other ministries can seem hands-off to an extent in their ways of equipping the church, where with pastors it is unmistakable that they are willing to get their hands dirty to see people healed and set free.

Since a pastor's job is so hands-on relationally, I think it is a practical statement to say that there should be one pastor to every twenty people or so. Those who aren't gifted pastorally, know that walking beside even one person who has a heart wound can be a challenging thing at times. I have a deep respect for large churches that have many pastors because I then know that the congregations' practical and emotional needs are taken into deep consideration. If pastors are taken out of the equation of the five-fold ministry, then neglect sneaks into churches and we can end up with a group of people who feel overlooked.

A true pastor will defend his or her sheep by any means necessary even if it means being blunt and straightforward at times. Shepherds can't always be gentle otherwise they won't do their job correctly in protecting the sheep. Actual shepherds hold a shepherding rod with a big cane on the end of it. If a sheep starts to wander away from the pack then the shepherd will put the rod around the sheep's neck to yank it back into line to protect it from being eaten by wolves. There has been a false teaching that has crept into the church saying that every leader needs to always be extremely nice in order to be Christ-like. To be kind and to be nice are two different things. Niceness isn't a fruit of the Spirit. Since this mindset has infected many leaders, those who look up to them have begun to walk in the same pattern which has brought passivity into the body. As long as we are passive, we will never be able to take care of what has been given to us. Adam made the same mistake when his bride Eve ate from the tree of knowledge of good and evil. Instead of embracing conflict and taking a stand to stop her, he became passive and just watched her eat the fruit.

As leaders we need to have a personality that reflects both The Lion and The Lamb. If we are only gentle like a lamb unable to confront the issues at hand, then people will undermine our authority in leadership and walk all over us. Not only will we be swept under the rug as leaders, but people will end up being pulled from truth by wolves and will end up getting hurt. That being said, if we are only bold and blunt like a lion then people will leave feeling hurt and wounded not by the wolves, but by us the leaders. There needs to be a healthy balance. Pastors need to protect the sheep from wolves and from undealt-with internal heart issues in great boldness just as much as they need to walk in a gentle representation of the Father to deal with such matters.

No matter who you are in the body of Christ, it is important to be under the covering of pastoral council in your relationships, work or ministry. There is a specific grace for pastors to understand matters of the heart so it's good to submit and be accountable, to have a second set of internal eyes to help examine what is happening in the realm of the soul. When we receive ministry from a true pastor not only will we become healthy emotionally, but we will also become pastoral ourselves. Since a pastor is called to train and equip the body of Christ, when we walk in relationship with a pastor and come under their mantle, we ourselves will begin to walk in the same anointing. This of course doesn't mean we ourselves are pastors, instead we will do the work of a pastor in the spheres of influence where God has entrusted us.

The Office Of An Evangelist

'The call of an evangelist' has been used very loosely in the church. We often label anyone who has a deep love for the lost an evangelist or say that they have the 'gift' of evangelism. Sorry to burst bubbles of comfort but there is no gift of evangelism, nor is everyone who loves the lost called as an evangelist. We are all called to love and reach the lost in the spheres of influence that God has given us.

I believe that there are two facets of ministry that evangelists will operate in. I say that there are commonly two facets because culture can determine at times how people will receive the gospel. The first stream or platform is when an evangelist is used as a direct spearhead to the mass population of the lost. These evangelists have an unusual favour with man from God and an incredible influence to impact the masses. These men and women are the Billy Graham, Oral Roberts and Reinhard Bonnke types. They are the ones who go where the gospel is scarce and have a favour with man resting upon them to draw people from everywhere to see mass salvations. This is where we can see we've gone wrong in terms of labelling everyone who does evangelism an evangelist. Our platform may only be in the lives of people in our schools or work places, where an evangelist will have platform from God with the masses.

There was a great acceleration of God raising up these types of evangelists during the Great Awakening which took place in the 1700 and 1800's. One of the men God rose up was John Wesley. He would stand under a tree and begin to share about the good news of Jesus as the masses would come to watch a man teaching about the cross and resurrection. Wonderful healings, deliverances and other manifestations of the Spirit would take place as he spoke. John had a strong revelation of impartation so he fathered hundreds of men to preach the gospel. Other men who flowed in this anointing, who are worth the time to study were George Whitefield, Jonathan Edwards, Charles Finney and D.L. Moody. These were all great men who diligently served the masses by laying down their lives for the gospel.

Presently we see a lot of these types of evangelists more commonly being released in third-world countries. God's heart is to still impact the masses in North America, but His strategy in using evangelists up here is different. Since media is so influential in our culture, a big crusade running all day throughout a Saturday won't draw people the same way here as it does in a place like Africa. Mass evangelists will spend time training and equipping others to do what they do, but their main outlet in ministry is to often be preaching the gospel in crusades.

In places like North America, the primary way to reach the masses is through large-scale training and equipping. The strategy is reversed. Instead of holding a big event that draws the people, the saints are trained and sent out to be Jesus everywhere they go, thus reaching the masses. This is where the second stream or platform of an evangelist comes in.

We are living in a time where the gospel is beginning to be presented to people in a tremendous way. Love for the broken and lost is starting to grip the church so tightly that we are coming to see the necessity of loving on people with the power of God. In order for us to walk in power we need the training and teaching. This is why we need evangelists. There are certain gifts like gifts of healing and word of knowledge that gravitate to evangelists because they are excellent tools to bring people into a direct love encounter with Jesus. Through impartation, evangelists are called to impart love and gifting such as these into the body of Christ so that His power and love can be established throughout the nations. Receiving the ministry of evangelists is crucial because their heart is to teach the church how to release the kingdom beyond the inner man.

The term evangelist was only placed on one or two men in the early church, as recorded in scripture. The first mention of an evangelist was Philip in Acts 21:8; "On the next day we who were Paul's companions departed and came to Caesarea, and entered the house of Philip the evangelist, who was one of the seven, and stayed with him." The second use of the term was concerning Timothy when Paul wrote him in 2 Timothy 4:5 saying; "Do the work of an evangelist, fulfill your ministry." The fact that Timothy wasn't called an evangelist and was instead told to do the work of an evangelist makes me question if he actually had the office calling. Since Timothy was discipled by Paul, I can assume that he too was apostolic and was being directed by Paul to step into the ministerial role of an evangelist for a time.

Evangelists have incredible anointing and purpose in leading people into becoming new creations in Christ. They are always moving as catalysts to birth revival. An evangelist's call is to birth, not to steward and mature. So, in order for them to have great effect they need to allow the rest of the body to follow up with the work that they are doing. Acts chapter 8 tells a story about how when Phillip the evangelist was preaching the gospel in Samaria, revival broke loose with salvations, baptisms, miracles, signs and wonders. When the apostles in Jerusalem heard that Samaria had received the Word of God through Philip, they sent Peter and John to begin to steward what God was doing. It is amazing to see how the evangelistic and apostolic ministries co-laboured together to see sustained revival. Philip as an evangelist taught the cross and resurrection with demonstrations of the Spirit's power and prepared the masses by baptizing them with the baptism of repentance. Afterwards the apostles stepped in to bring the masses to maturity by laying hands on them to receive Holy Spirit. We can even see how Peter began to disciple a former sorcerer that Philip had earlier converted.

An evangelist's work always needs to be overseen and followed up by apostles, otherwise the move of God will die out due to a lack of proper leadership. Although some of his theologies are highly controversial, John Calvin was an incredible reformer who pushed forth God's work. As an apostle, he partnered with an evangelist named Guillaume Farel. Farel would go forth spreading the news of the kingdom and John positioned himself to follow him to nurture what Farel had birthed. Where Farel would preach, John would raise up leaders to take care of what Farel had started.

There is a great restlessness that can take over evangelists to see the broken and lost set free. Since the drive is great they will at times run ahead of the body. Although they run ahead, it's important that they don't run so far that they are disconnected, otherwise their fruit will only be Christians who haven't learned to grow beyond infancy. This office, just as with all the others can't operate properly independently. Part of the call is learning how to trust others to take care of what they themselves have started.

The Office Of A Prophet

One of the functions of a prophet is to be God's mouthpiece within the place of influence given to him or her. A prophet will have an unusual favour like not many have to speak into the ears of men and women of influence. When we look in the Old Testament, we see that the prophets were given great platforms to speak God's word. Isaiah was a counsellor to kings, Micaiah had such favour that kings would come to him to oversee their strategy for war. The same will be for New Testament prophets. They may have platform that allows them to speak to people like government leaders, big business owners or influential leaders of the church. We can see that the New Testament prophet takes on some of the roles of the Old Testament prophet. However, their function in ministry differs greatly. This is very important to note. I have met many people who have had legitimate calls to the office of a prophet, but they would try to minister as though they are Old Testament prophets in New Testament times. God doesn't have a doom and gloom message as in the time before the cross. We aren't living under the ministry of death anymore so the message isn't death. We are living in revival times so His message is life and love.

As I mentioned before in the 'Spirit Man' section, one of the prophet's main functions is to deposit into the church the things that come naturally to a prophet. This is one of the main things that separates an O.T. prophet from a N.T. prophet. Back before the cross there were numerous prophets, but there were only two accounts recorded in biblical history which promotes the thought of the prophets of old training and equipping other people to move in the prophetic. The first account is in 1 Samuel 10, where it mentions the concession of prophets that prophesied with Saul. It is very possible that this group of prophets were trained and risen up through Samuel's ministry. The second account is in 1 and 2 Kings, where there is mention of many prophets destroying the works of darkness. Taking the numbers into consideration, it can be safely assumed that there must have been select prophets who were mentoring and discipling in this time. Elijah and Elisha's relationship are a good confirmation of this. Where in the O.T. this form of discipleship was scarce, every N.T. prophet that God raises up today has a job to train and equip the saints in doing what comes naturally to him.

Just as the title 'evangelist' has been taken out of context, so has the calling of 'prophet'. Not everyone who prophesies and hears God's voice is a prophet. All of us are called to hear God's voice and speak His word because we have received Holy Spirit who searches the deep things of God. In the O.T. prophets would stand apart, seeming mystical and almost intimidating. Since man had no spiritual grid, prophets were seen as separate from the nations and from the house of Israel. However, because of the cross, a prophet is no longer separate, he is made one with the body of Christ. His job is to demystify the prophetic and prophetic experience by establishing a prophetic culture within the church. A prophet will show the accessibility and commonality of God's voice since we are all now in direct relationship with Holy Spirit.

Receiving the ministry of prophets is essential in our journey of being fathered and mothered. We need to know how to hear and discern God's voice, so that we can speak His word wherever He has called us. We also need prophets to teach us how to experience God in prophetic encounters, because when we can learn to position ourselves to encounter God in the secret place, we are transformed into His likeness. The Bible shares many prophetic encounters that prophets have had, whether they were third-heaven encounters, encounters with the angelic, visions, dreams or out-of-body experiences. Such things are a prophet's inheritance. Just as they are his or her inheritance to receive, it is also an inheritance that is intended by God to be deposited within the church.

Although prophets will quickly gravitate to co-labouring with apostles because these two ministries greatly compliment one another, a prophet's ministry will be properly balanced out in partnering with teachers and pastors. Since I've always gravitated to equipping and activating people in this particular realm, I have seen many different mindsets that can creep up on prophetic people. This is an essential nugget of wisdom for anyone who feels a prophetic calling over their lives: receive from prophets to sharpen your ears, but make sure you keep around teachers so that you never stray from the written Word of God. It can be a dangerous thing when someone begins to believe that the Now Prophetic word stands in greater authority than the written Word of God. I always tell everyone that I train to prophesy, that if they want to grow to reach maturity in speaking the prophetic word of God, they need to be deeply rooted in the written Word of God.

When we are receiving from prophets it is also good for a prophetic person to be around pastors to keep them down to earth. Where a prophet will teach people to see God in the heavens, a pastor will help people to see God in relationships. Where a prophet is called to develop one's spirit, the pastor nurtures the soul. This again points back to the truth of being well-rounded in our three-fold being. A prophetic person needs the ministry of the rest of the body or there can be a temptation to fall into a mindset of gnosticism. Gnosticism is simply dismissing the importance of anything that isn't potently supernatural or spiritual. It is important to develop our spirits, but we also need to be mature in our souls, otherwise we can undermine our identity as emotional beings, making us live like spiritual robots. This way of thinking can lead someone to dismiss the responsibility of being a good spouse, son, daughter, or friend.

In the New Testament there are many mentionings of people who clearly walked in the office calling of a prophet. However, there were only mention of three people who were actually named and called N.T. prophets.

Acts 15:32; "Now Judas and Silas, themselves being prophets also, exhorted and strengthened the brethren with many words."

166

Acts 21:10; "And as we stayed many days, a certain prophet named Agabus came down from Judea."

God brought an acceleration of understanding of the prophetic office back to the church in 1988. At first, since it was a new revelation there was some wisdom that needed to be learned in how to steward this new revelation properly. As with most truths that are restored, some people took the revelation to an extreme and allowed their zeal to cause some damage before wisdom had the chance to catch up to it. After some mistakes were made, people feared prophets and dismissed the entire move of God as something that wasn't even from Holy Spirit. We should never make decisions out of fear. Just because a few mistakes were made, we shouldn't throw away the blessings with the curses. We instead need to embrace the move of God and receive His fire which will refine the ministry. God is raising up a prophetic generation throughout the nations who will unashamedly speak His word. The ministry of prophets needs to be received and honoured in order for this movement to advance from infancy to adulthood. Refined prophets will be able to set up the proper boundaries that will guard the saints from falling into some of the ditches that many have fallen into in the past. Their fathering and mothering within the church will create a healthy community of people who hear and know their Father's voice.

The Office Of An Apostle

I remember when I first gave my heart to the Lord, I was drawn to studying Paul the apostle's ministry. However, since I had a lack of teaching on church leadership, I was unaware of what an apostle actually was. So, after church one day, I approached my pastor at the time, hoping that he would shed some light on my current curiosity. I greeted him with what I thought was simple a question by asking him what an apostle was; after I asked, my pastor looked over at me blankly and responded by saying; "Luc, I honestly have no clue."

Out of the entire five-fold ministry, the role of an apostle has been the most misunderstood by the church. Since the call has been misunderstood for so long, not only has it been casually overlooked, it has in a lot of ways been completely forgotten. This is why the myth which says that apostles were only for the early church crept into some of our doctrine, when really, if we understood the role of the apostolic ministry we would quickly understand its importance and would be quick to embrace it.

An apostle's heart is to create a place where God's presence can rest and remain. I don't mean this in the sense that an apostle will just buy a building and set in motion some good programs, hoping that it will gravitate the glory. An apostle's job is to form Christ within the church (the people) so that they can stretch beyond adolescence and into maturity (Galatians 4:19). As each individual within the church grows up and comes into a further revelation of what was accomplished at the cross and resurrection, God's glory and kingdom will be manifest wherever the church goes. This is the type of spiritual building that attracts God's presence. It is a building constructed of living stones, not natural ones. Other than Jesus, Paul was probably the greatest apostle who had ever lived. Like all apostles, he had a territorial anointing. Where pastors love the individual and dream for the individual, apostles love the individual but dream for the nations.

An apostle is kind of like the manager of a store. Where some people might be an expert in specific areas of the store, their understanding won't stretch beyond their station, whereas an apostle understands the full functioning of every job that makes the store flow and work. Since this is the case, apostles are usually very universally gifted. They also have a grace to weave in and out of specific calls and anointings if necessary to complete their mandate. Throughout Acts and the Epistles that Paul wrote we can see pretty clearly how Paul as an apostle operated. Again, take into consideration that this isn't a in-depth teaching on the apostolic, but is a brief overview of the call.

Paul, although an apostle, would often go to a region first functioning in the role of an evangelist. He would preach the gospel, heal the sick, raise the dead and cast out demons. When people were birthed into salvation he would then pick a few that he saw as potential leaders and begin to father them. As an expert builder, Paul would build and form Christ within those he was fathering through his teachings so that he could later appoint them within the church. We can see now, that here he would begin to operate in more of the call of a teacher and would also pastor those he discipled. As I've said, apostles will often understand the full functioning of the store and will for a time step into different roles when necessary.

Often prophets and apostles will work together in these beginning stages of the church. Whenever there is a work to be done with the foundation God will use the apostles and prophets.

Ephesians 2:19-20 - "Now, therefore, you are no longer strangers and foreigners, but fellow citizens with the saints and members of the household of God, having been built on the foundation of the apostles and prophets."

After a few leaders were raised up under Paul, he would begin to station them within the church that he was birthing. The apostles and prophets would then discern who fits where for the church plant. The story of Noah is symbolically an excellent parallel of how an apostle is to use the church body's diversity. Just as Noah built a boat that had a place for every species of animal and its mate, an apostle is to place people where their gifts can be used for the kingdom in a way that will bring multiplication. It didn't matter to Noah how different one animal was from the other, Noah had a place prepared for each within the boat. It's interesting to note that we aren't called to be 'living bricks' to build a spiritual house, but instead are called as living stones. Bricks are easy to place on top of one another because they are in the shape of rectangles, where stones come in all shapes and sizes. It takes an expert to put a variety of awkwardly-shaped stones together with the intent of seeing them work together for a common purpose. An apostle knows that there is a place in the body of Christ for every gift, calling, mantle, anointing and talent. As people are released by the apostle to minister in the church in whatever area they're passionate about, more ministries and leaders will begin to pop up, expanding the vision of the church's purpose. In doing this, the people as a whole become a massive bridge that ushers heaven to earth in the realm where they are anointed to operate.

Apostles live to see what is happening in heaven established on the earth. An apostle steps into barren land and creates a dwelling place for God that is made of people from the bottom up. At first, things look messy and the apostle is running around trying to make everything work, but in the end after everyone is raised up and appointed, he gets to step back and see an organic wineskin functioning and operating on its own. Essentially, the apostle works himself out of a job so that he can begin to build elsewhere. When an apostle is present, those who lead under his or her covering will begin to flow in an apostolic anointing to manage and steward. This is essential, otherwise all of the ministries that were birthed through the apostle remain co-dependant on him instead of becoming self-sustaining. Although an apostle may begin building in another place, he will often take a place of governing and overseeing the move of God that was set in motion through him. We can see how even though Paul planted in many different places, he was constantly writing the churches and playing the role of a father to the churches that he had raised up.

Without the apostles' hands working within the formation of the emerging church, the body will go without proper governing and order. Individuals within the church wouldn't be able to walk in the fullness of their potential because there is confusion about where they fit. The presence of an apostle deposits a sense of purpose, since they carry a revelation that everyone is a leader in God's kingdom.

The Age Of The Seraphim

Recently, I was standing in heaven with Jesus. While I was with Him, He didn't display the image of Jesus the Shepherd or Jesus the Rabbi. Instead, I saw Him as the Commander and General of all heaven's army. His very presence was at the same time both noble and daunting. Stationed as an unshakable pillar, He radiated integrity and wisdom that would have demanded respect from the greatest of kings. He spoke to me in a calm tone that held unmatched authority saying, "Fourteen years ago, I sent the cherubim to earth to minister to all believers that would receive their ministry. In this next season I will send forth My seraphim, to usher a new age of restored identity to the saints."

Now, there is an important message that we need to extract from this experience. In order to do that, we are first going to take a brief look at the cherubim. The cherubim are angels that were mentioned in Ezekiel 1. If you read through the chapter you will get a full description from Ezekiel of their heavenly appearance. Although their appearance is worth describing or even teaching on, the part that I want to highlight about them is the aspect of God which they encountered. Ezekiel writes about how the cherubim were constantly standing in the presence of God, seeing and encountering Him first and foremost in the depiction of His glory.

Ezekiel 1:26-28 says; "Above the firmament over their (the cherubim's) heads was the likeness of a throne, in appearance of a sapphire stone; on the likeness of a throne was a likeness with the appearance of a man high above it. Also from the appearance of His waist and upward I saw, as it were, the colour of amber with the appearance of fire all around within it; and from the appearance of His waist and downward I saw, as it were, the appearance of fire with brightness all around. Like the appearance of a rainbow in a cloud on a rainy day, so was the appearance of the brightness all around it. *This was the appearance of the likeness of the glory of the Lord*."

Since the cherubim were in a continuous state of basking in God's glory, when they were sent to the earth, they ministered to the saints by revealing a new level of His glory. The cherubim simply presented to the church, the heavenly culture to which they were accustomed. I believe that this is part of the reason why there has been such a swift acceleration of the increase in understanding of His glory in these past years. Since this revelation has been received by much of the church, as the global body, we have continued to advance into its greater revelatory depth ever since.

Now, lets look at the seraphim:

Isaiah 6:1-2; "In the year that King Uzziah died, I saw the Lord sitting on a throne, high and lifted up, and the train of His robe filled the temple. Above it stood seraphim; each one had six wings: with two he covered his face, with two he covered his feet, and with two he flew."

Where the cherubim were constantly encountering God the King of glory, the seraphim were stationed to soak in the presence of God the King of kings. I say this because back in the Old Testament, when a king would claim new land the train of his robe would be lengthened, symbolizing the new expansion of the territory that he governed. Since Jesus' robe in Isaiah 6 was so long that it filled the temple, it speaks of His never-ending authority not only throughout the nations, but also of His complete majesty over every aspect of creation. He is the King of kings. Heaven is His throne and the earth is His footstool. All authority and power has been given to Him.

Since the time has come for the seraphim to descend to the earth, we can be confident to believe that we are embarking upon a new age, where a greater depth of confidence will be restored within the bride's identity. I believe that as the seraphim are commissioned to the earth, they will deposit an understanding of the King of kings. They will minister a revelation revealing that we are all called to co-reign with Jesus as kings and queens over everything that He Himself has received from the Father. We are transformed in His glory, but we can only properly host it when we learn that we are called to govern the land which it has descended upon. It is our responsibility to stand as kings and queens to tend the land, making it a proper dwelling place for heaven. The seraphim's descent to earth is going to result in revelatory wisdom in the body of Christ concerning how to steward a revival that will ride throughout the nations. However, before that can happen, the first fruit of their ministry will be a generation who has first learned to reign within the garden of the inner man.

The culture that you create internally for yourself is the culture that people will experience every time they encounter you. It is a wonderful gift from God that we get to grow as quickly as we are willing to receive. The hungrier that we allow ourselves to become will determine how much food we get to eat, since God promises to always satisfy. That being said, I have built a ladder of truths for you to climb at whatever pace you choose. Your maximum potential height is endless as you ascend closer towards an eternal God who loves you. As you grow towards Him, Jesus the Son will continue to be formed within you, creating an irresistible dwelling place for heaven.

I will finish by saying that I took the time to write this book because I believe in every one of you who are reading my words right now. I believe in who you are called to be because God has designed you with a specific and unique purpose. You have all of heaven's support behind whatever God calls you to do. Right now, I bless you to receive as sons and daughters. I bless you to learn as students who are teachable. I bless you to reign as kings and queens in the inner land, and beyond to wherever God may call you.

You are God's garden. You are His place of pleasure.

You are highly blessed and favoured. Your Daddy God is proud of you. You are His delight. He loves you just the way you are. He believes in your dreams. You are so beautiful to Him. You are brilliant. You are so precious, so priceless, so loved.